Continuing
Higher
Education
The Coming Wave

Continuing Higher Education
The Coming Wave

Editors
Allan W. Lerner
B. Kay King

 TEACHERS COLLEGE PRESS

Teachers College, Columbia University
New York and London

Published by Teachers College Press, 1234 Amsterdam Avenue
New York, New York

Library of Congress Cataloging-in-Publication Data

Continuing higher education : the coming wave / editors, Allan W.
  Lerner, B. Kay King.
     p.   cm.
  Includes bibliographical references and indexes.
  ISBN 0-8077-3197-8 (alk.)
  1. Continuing education. 2. Education, Higher. I. Lerner, Allan
W. II. King, B. Kay.
LC5215.C68   1992
374 – dc20   92-24511

ISBN 0-8077-3197-8

Printed on acid-free paper

Manufactured in the United States of America

99 98 97 96 95 94 93 92   8 7 6 5 4 3 2 1

Contents

Acknowledgments

A book of this type, which offers a new point of view, is inevitably the product of many beneficial exposures to the thinking of scholars and practitioners representing a variety of disciplines and experiences. On the shoulders of these relationships, something "new" may eventually emerge. So it has been in the development of the ideas that have gone into this work; so we are pleased to offer several acknowledgements. We have benefited greatly from the stimulating forums which NUCEA has provided to a number of the contributors to this volume over the years. The annual programs on leadership, curriculum, marketing and demographic issues related to continuing education have served to challenge and support us in the process of bringing our ideas and recommendations into focus. Similarly, our students and practitioner associates who have sought continuing education relationships with our universities have shown us, time and again, that the ultimate product of our efforts can be so intrinsically valuable to its final audiences that the frustrations and uncertainties which often surround new approaches to important tasks are well worth enduring, even at their most difficult moments. Finally, we must acknowledge those supportive executive administrators at our institutions who have arisen at the crucial moments in the development of our more ambitious undertakings, to provide the leadership upon which all our visions for continuing education are ultimately dependent.

In each of these circles of colleagues the list of those deserving mention is lengthy. However, we must note at least a few by name at this point. Our special thanks to all of the following for each of their contributions, made in their own ways, to our collective efforts: Robert L. Bender, Genivee Carter, Charles V. Evans, Karen R. Hitchcock, Richard M. Johnson, Kay Kohl, Mary L. Pankowski, Veerasamy K. G. Pillay, Clara Ringo, Paul D. Scheels, Steven L. Schomberg, Robert G. Simerly, Vanessa A. Taylor, James C. Votruba, John A. Wanat, James E. Weigand, and Ward W. Weldon.

1

The Coming Wave

Allan W. Lerner

This book describes how continuing education—as a structure and a function—can become a unique tool for reorienting major universities to confront new societal challenges. My colleagues and I have called these challenges "the coming wave."

Growing up on Coney Island, I learned early on that a swimmer facing a coming wave can and should have a general idea of what is about to happen, and of how to take advantage of it when it does. I also concluded very early on, while waiting in my inner tube, that (1) not having a plan in the face of an approaching wave resulted in a mouth full of sand and seaweed—or worse; but that (2) if I turned my back on the wave, it would come anyway, often seeming to hit harder; so that (3) picking the right inner tube is very important; and (4) when my friends and I chose to venture out, it was armed with a good plan and appreciation of good timing.

Experience suggests that a career in higher education is not that different from a day of facing waves at Coney Island. This book explains how that is so, for the following chapters are concerned with a series of formidable changes about to break over institutions of higher education. We are particularly concerned with the very large, multifaceted, multipurpose institutions struggling to maintain a coherent whole at least as great as the sum of their parts—the "mega-universities." These are the comprehensive research universities, many public but some private, typified, on the whole, by the membership of the National Association of State Universities and Land Grant Colleges.

Having been recognized for their research, these institutions are now coming under fire to solve social problems. This is especially true of public universities, which are funded by the state. Because they are dependent on the taxpayer, such institutions face particular pressure to provide significant assistance on social policy issues. Health, education, reindustrialization, crime, race relations, gender injustice, political participation, and the salvaging of traditional family values (if not structures as well) are some of the social problem areas which the mega-universities are expected to address directly.

Thus, for example, industry and government expect that the mega-universities will produce applied research that can be used to restore competitiveness with Japan and fend off Western Europe. Universities feel the pressure to facilitate technology development, to experiment in social reform, and even to replace social institutions, as in the case of failed public school systems.

Responding to these pressures demands new skills and activities; meanwhile, the traditional student pool is declining. The latter development makes it more difficult for the university to cling to its conventional educational role, even if it were inclined to ignore external pressures for practical assistance in public policy formulation and implementation.

To be sure, movement out of any steady state is relatively inefficient and creates its own organizational turbulence in addition to the environmental turbulence that prompted the organizational change. Thus, mega-universities, developed as research institutions (with conventional teaching and service activities legitimated but not always emphasized), now face external demographic and attitudinal shifts that cause internal vibration as well. The pressures produce resistance as well as attempts at responsiveness. Answers must be fashioned that address these pressures without turning the institution on its ear.

A basic premise of this volume is that a rethought continuing education function, with the development of attendant new continuing education structures, can be used to accomplish the needed adjustments without sacrificing the research commitment of the mega-university, and without the radical internal changes advocated by some external critics. In the long term, continuing education can become the medium for a new synthesis of traditional research excellence with partially reoriented teaching and revitalized public service based on sophisticated interinstitutional relationships. This includes more significant interaction not only with noneducational institutions but with four-year colleges and community colleges.

These smaller institutions are better suited to providing the traditional service functions, undergraduate extension curriculum, and introductory training programs which have fallen under the heading of continuing education. As the mega-university adapts to new developments, and in so doing reconceptualizes the continuing education function and its structures, the continuing education terrain it abandons will be populated by smaller institutions with which it should maintain a close working relationship in a true spirit of public service.

In any event, many of the adjustments that public-spiritedness would recommend, survival in good health will require. For the mega-universities present a broad profile to the coming wave; they are large targets offering considerable resistance. Their heels are well dug in, and they are not going to be swept away easily. But neither can they hope to bob painlessly on the surface, oblivious to the hard slam followed by the powerful undertow. The price of these institutions' significance is that they always have much at stake, and cannot afford to float blithely, even if they were small and simple enough to be capable of doing so — which they are not. They have no choice but to face what confronts them; they need an attitude of preparedness, a strategy, and tactical choices, if they are to experience what is coming as a natural force whose energy can be harnessed.

The alternative to proactive adaptation is to stand frozen, content to be victimized, ready with irony and excuses, traumatically overwhelmed by an irresistible force. Institutions that do so may find their research funding dwindling, or coming from corporate sources that impose unscholarly restrictions on research practice and dissemination. Also possible are restricted capital budgets, intervention in self-governance, reduced operating budgets, pressures to accept a "consumerist" culture of education, and all the pain that comes from being perceived as weak in performing one's organizational mission, and resistant to "accountability," as measured by the uninitiated.

To meet the coming challenge, these modern, large-scale, multicollege mega-universities will require visionary leadership fused with superb management predicated on thorough self-knowledge and understanding of environmental dynamics. Universities committed to service, teaching, and research will need to integrate these functions and genuinely excel at all three in order to deal with a changing environment. They will need to hone the capacity to establish and pursue new lines of institutional self-development; they will need to develop the capacity for spiraled growth into the future.

Their fundamental institutional values will always have to be enacted in full acknowledgment of the established cycles of academic activity, but these cycles must be carried on in new contexts. The cyclical pattern must take account of the future; the circle must become a spiral. The spiral must remain intact through several, conspicuously different environmental media.

Modern universities, and especially mega-universities, must confront a market of academic competitors, potential limited partners from the corporate sector, other organizational clients and educational "consumers," and third parties influencing the disposition of such clients. These range from political movements to graduate student unions. They have significant relations with foreign nations; national, state, and local governments; the corporate world; their communal neighbors; institutions fashioning "inputs" to the universities; institutions receiving the "outputs" of the universities; partially substitutable institutions; the third sector; and institutions of popular culture.

Consider, for example, the frequency with which the national media focus on what were formerly the internal, seemingly arcane matters of academic politics, university administrative succession, and campus life. National newspapers now report on disputes over indirect costs formulas, tenure processes, free-speech issues raised by student newspapers, and university fundraising policies. The front page of the *New York Times* occasionally reads like the *Chronicle of Higher Education*. Not since medieval times have the goings-on within the academic buildings been such a curiosity to the townspeople. The recent era of relative isolation seems to be passing. The threat is not from drunkards with pickaxes; it is from the consequences of ignoring a dissolving boundary between internal and external. Higher and thicker walls were a sensible solution to the torch processions that not so long ago confronted the academy. In light of the current changes, however, walls are not a solution; they are part of the problem. The solution lies in anticipating and responding to changes in the institutional atmosphere while continuing to embody and expound core educational values.

The following chapters each support and build upon this notion. To remain vibrant, the university, especially the mega-university, must change its way of preserving its essence. As Joe Donaldson and Jovita Ross-Gordon indicate in Chapter 2, the university must adapt to a fundamentally altered student body. Marcia Escott, William Semlak, and Mark Comadena explain how a modified university mission will affect university faculty (Chapter 3). Joe Donaldson considers how such developments will influence the research agenda (Chapter 4). Chapter 5 consists of an essay Kay King and I published on what may be described here as the strengths and weaknesses of various continuing education models—the suitability of various structural arrangements for delivering continuing education through universities. Our point is that strategically informed decisions on continuing education structure are necessary in light of preferences for various functional orientations. Kay King's chapter on financial strategies (Chapter 6) explains how the mega-university can adapt to a changing financial context in which entrepreneurism must be given its due without being given centrality. Finally, in Chapter 7, I try to explain how the modern university must prepare for a changing relationship with external organizations in an environment that is essentially a complicated web of organizations.

Indeed, all the essays in this volume assume that continuing education is an ideal vehicle for universities determined to take an aggressive stance toward the coming wave. It is, so to speak, the inner tube of choice. Hence our title: *Continuing Higher Education: The Coming Wave of Change.*

Further, these essays share the belief that continuing education's strategic value is its inherent suitability to university dealings at the now dissolving boundary with the environment. Why else has it been called "extension education"? We are aware that redefining "extension" entails considerable "post-stereotypical" thinking about continuing education. But, given all that university executives will have to do to face the next decade successfully, it is no longer unrealistic to expect that they will also have to reconceptualize continuing education and gain a new appreciation of its use in furthering an institutional strategy intended to master profound environmental changes.

Unfortunately, the new challenges to institutional leadership will have to be met with little help from existing wisdom. The irony of academic administration is that most existing theories of administration and organization do not apply in this situation; most theories of university governance fail to take account of the changing context that the coming wave will create.

Most existing theories of administration have as their implied referent the Weberian bureaucracy. That is, they are developed with a conceptual orientation that is concerned with big, entrenched, lumbering, often inefficient but ineradicable, trial-and-error-oriented organizations.

Most theories of university governance are entrenched in the traditional rhetoric of pristine pursuit of knowledge in an environment that is passive, stable, quaint, and adequate if not munificent. Chronic, structurally significant, environmental turbulence is alien to the assumptions of traditional models of modern university administration (Lynton & Elman, 1987).

One reason why the coming wave will feel like more than a mere ripple is that modern mega-universities cannot withstand failures in their own performance as easily as they have five, three, or even two decades ago. They are structurally far less tolerant of mistakes. The mega-university can no longer easily settle for a casual "win some, lose some" posture toward its tasks and its environments.

To use the terminology of environmental description suggested by Katz and Kahn (1978), the environment is more turbulent than stable, more diverse than uniform, more scarce than munificent, and more clustered than random. In the latter regard, formidable blocs of interest must now be dealt with, rather than dispersed, ad hoc voices posing little organized challenge.

As large organizations, universities have been viewed in Weick's (1979) and Cohen and March's (1986) terms as loosely linked organizations. They are hard to mobilize from the top, hard to plan with, hard to "control." They have a capacity for resilience, but this is not the same as an anticipatory, fast-reaction capability. Indeed, from an organization theory perspective, it is unclear whether the resilience of loose linkage can be turned into a capacity for high-performance, quick-reaction, low-error conduct under stressful conditions.

More and more, however, the mega-university may have to increase its capability for both resilience and high performance. The future will require increased capacity for both. In broadest terms, we are entering a period when universities cannot afford to tolerate failure or settle for mediocrity. This will compress the effect of the changes demanded by the demographic and social shifts that characterize the coming wave.

The following discussion of relevant organization theory should help to explain the special role of continuing education in this context, and to amplify the relationship between what we call the coming wave and what we see as the nature of the mega-university.

RESILIENCE, HIGH PERFORMANCE, AND THE MEGA-UNIVERSITY STRUCTURE

Mega-universities, with their costly physical plants, their dependence on competitive, research-focused, external funding and on declining sources of fixed income, their competition for students and from non-academic institutions of research, consulting, and education, are no longer able to operate successfully as traditional bureaucracies. That is, they cannot be content with a standard operating procedure in which many errors may occur, with the solution being to reperform the erroneous act correctly, if and when the deviation from standard procedure comes to light. This approach is as anachronistic in higher education administration as static, high-casualty trench warfare is in modern battle.

Unfortunately, the doctrines of administrative theory for large organizations — especially large public organizations — seem to encourage outdated frameworks of assumptions. They stress economy and accountability, not resiliency, rapid adjustment, and high performance. True, a recent spate of management theory has focused on the concepts of organizational culture and of executive intervention in, and deliberate modification of, such organizational cultures (Ott, 1989; Peters & Waterman, 1982; Scott & Hart, 1989). However, much of this material fails to link its focus on social psychological climate and rewards manipulation to deeper issues of organizational design, structure-function associations, institutional-environmental interpenetration, and system transformations, institutional "learning," and "self-correction" (Weick, 1979; Matejko, 1986). While the social psychological climate, as an aspect of the organizational system, is a significant factor in organizational performance, it certainly cannot be viewed in isolation when seeking to understand or effect significant organizational transformation, or to maintain a given organizational state in a changing environment. It is unfortunate that tampering with organizational culture has been a fashionable panacea in much of the popular and some of the academic literature lately.

This state of affairs complicates the task of executive leadership of mega-universities, because it means that most administrative theory does not fit the problem, the institution, or the underlying currents of institutional processes. Most of the solutions proffered by administrative and managerial sciences do not apply to today's problems, or never did suit the peculiarities of the institution very well, or are superficial. Guidance must be gleaned from the exceptions. This is true for many organizations that will need to sustain prolonged periods of—indeed, an operational orientation toward—continuous high performance. It is also true for organizations of the loosely linked variety, such as universities, which never did fit classic administrative theories, even in more leisurely times.

LaPorte and Consolini (1991) writes:

> There is little systematic theoretical or empirical work on the dynamics of those modern organization[s] whose members (and the public) perceive that operational failures could result in increasingly dangerous and harmful consequences. This situation need not be problematic if HROs [high-reliability organizations] differed little from those trial-and-error organizations that are "failure tolerant," that is, they operate systems for which production failures are not likely to result in costly consequences and where the value of the lessons so learned is greater than the cost of making them. . . . Yet organization theory literature rarely speaks to this situation. This literature has been derived almost exclusively from organizations in which trial-and-error learning is the predominant and accepted mode of learning and improvement. Contemporary administrative/organization theories are essentially theories of trial-and-error, failure-tolerant, low-reliability organizations. For the rare exceptions see Landau (1969, 1973), Lerner (1986), Lustick (1980), and Woodhouse (1988) for a beginning logic that calls for empirical work. (p. 22)

LaPorte and Consolini go on to list three characteristics distinguishing HROs from conventional organizations. I would suggest that only one of the three is problematic in seeking to analogize to mega-universities facing the coming wave, and that, moreover, the problem of fit essentially dissolves on closer inspection. My point is that HRO capabilities are necessary for mega-universities that wish to cope effectively with future demands. More broadly, I am suggesting that if HRO capabilities are to be expected of loosely linked organizations, special burdens will fall upon their executive leadership. For executives of mega-universities, one of the best-suited and most powerful tools will prove to be continuing education—as structural device and functional initiative—for reasons which will be further elaborated here.

Consider now LaPorte and Consolini's (1991) three distinguishing features of HROS:

1. Increasingly, the physical technologies and their organizational operating units are tightly coupled so that if important elements in routine production processes fail, the organization's capacity to perform at all is severely threatened. Failure of a component causes such damage that the capacity of the organization to perform is threatened altogether.
2. The results of operational failures are visible and increasingly feared by the public, which perceives, therefore, that it has a very high stake in assuring failure-free operation. Strong public, external pressures exist for very reliable internal operations, not only for overall performance or economic profit.
3. These HROs have, until recently, had relatively abundant resources, allowing them to invest heavily in reliability-enhancing activities. This has nurtured an organizational perspective in which short-term efficiency has taken second seat to very high-reliability operations. (pp. 22–23)

Regarding the second compound descriptor, the mega-university is already under increasing pressure to do everything from fixing the public school system to reversing global warming. At the same time, there is decreasing tolerance for alleged research boondoggling, training the foreign competition, and providing unlimited medical care for the indigent. Even the core instructional operations (including teaching undergraduates), which are almost prosaic when compared to uniquely mega-university activities such as basic research and high technology development, are now under hyperscrutiny associated with the consumerist perspective of the public and the political perspective of special publics.

Both public and private universities are becoming publicly scrutinized institutions, and public mega-universities are especially vulnerable in a volatile social and political environment. External pressures are significantly greater than they were even a few years ago. Few mega-university executives can operate under the assumption that there is general tolerance of operational failures.

Regarding LaPorte and Consolini's third characteristic, mega-universities and, indeed, higher education belong to an institutional culture in which recent and impending hard times are presented as a sea change compared to the postwar formative period of more casual university financing and hence of laxer spending and accountability habits. Here too, the climate of the modern mega-university can be likened to that of an HRO.

The first characteristic of HROs reflects a common theme in the few sources that have dealt with the special character of ostensibly fail-safe organizations and the nature of the situations that bring them down or come close to doing so. This is the general idea of a series of compounded errors so tightly sequenced that even modest deviations can suddenly create a cyclone of a problem.

Perrow (1984) stressed that rapidly compounding deviations in such situations often were unforeseeable, seemingly "oddball" combinations of circumstances that defied anticipation or diagnosis while they were occurring. Sense-making would only be possible in a postmortem. Further, he suggested that such errors were most likely where the core technology of the organization was fundamentally mysterious to the operatives, who had, shall we say, managed to harness the process without exactly understanding it or controlling it.

When we meld Perrow's perspective with LaPorte and Consolini's, HRO-like vulnerabilities appear as objectively demanding performance complexities and rapidities combined with subjective limits in cognitively processing what the organizational task would appear to demand.

The usual empirical subjects in studies of such conditions are more likely to be air traffic controllers and nuclear power plant operators than university executives. However, the comparison is perhaps not so farfetched after all, for the essence of an HRO is that it cannot afford to fail and cannot take its time; it is coping with a rapid barrage of environmental stimuli in a game that "takes no prisoners."

While mega-universities facing the coming decade are not dealing with the tightly coupled problems facing nuclear power plants or air traffic controllers, they are confronting complex pressures, considerable hazards of error, one-shot opportunities to act or blow a situation, external groups that will not wait for the report of a faculty committee yet to be appointed, costly systemic damage as a constant danger, and problems involving unit activities that are impenetrable and volatile. Illustrations range from press-conference pressures and legislative ultimata to alumni complaints and corporate overtures for contract research and project co-development.

The coming wave represents the swift increase in such pressures, which, it is suggested here, will require something on the order of HRO behavior by university leaders if a successful organizational adjustment is to be made. The mega-universities that ride the coming wave successfully will be those that learn to perform more like HROs.

The stress on mega-universities will be caused by a sharp move in the HRO direction on a continuum that places the mega-university somewhere between a teachers' college of the 1950s and an aircraft carrier in combat. The crucial point will be a sudden jump toward the model of the latter after a history of relative stability.

HRO CAPABILITY AND LOOSELY COUPLED STRUCTURE

Earlier, it was noted that universities are the traditional examples of *loosely coupled organizations* (Weick, 1978; March & Olsen, 1976; Cohen & March, 1986). Generally, the term applies to organizations lacking hierarchical accountability. In loosely coupled organizations, units have a high degree of autonomy of function. The couplings between them are relatively modest, and are flexible. These units — like academic departments, centers, institutes, programs, schools, and colleges, within a mega-university — are given relative autonomy. The larger administrative structure of managerial actors remains relatively distant from the decisions and activities of the subunits. In universities these include issues such as what and how to teach, what to research and what to conclude, whom to provide with "service" (whatever that actually means), what grants to apply for with proposals containing what research plan, whom to flunk, and so on.

Exponents of the concept of loosely coupled organizations have stressed the consequences of low operational control by a central organizational authority. However, as Meyer and Rowan (1983) explain, the primary environmental demand on educational institutions is not for the functions that remain loosely coupled. Rather, it is for credentialing from educational institutions so as to enable graduates to assume social roles.

From institutions of higher education, and mega-universities in particular, we may expect more than social certification of graduates. These institutions also offer multiple credentialing, assistance, and research products. Nonetheless, in general terms, loose linkage means that hierarchic officials are distanced from internal core functions and their daily activities. This does not, however, mean that they are removed from the demands on the institution as a whole, or that they cannot respond to environmental pressures for products, programs, and services *by that whole*. These offerings include institution-to-institution arrangements for educational programs; consulting; public-service consortium arrangements; research products, programs, or even partnerships; and so on. The point is that while the content of such activities as conducted by faculty and graduate students is not controlled by the university or the receiving organization, the strategic decisions to undertake such programs, and the institutional commitments to see them through, are made formally by the university. More precisely, the university had better take charge at the strategic level, or the arrangements will not be made, and the mega-university will find itself out of step with a new environment.

Thus, in the functional domains that are of significance to the larger, external organizational environment, there exist both the need and the capability for centralized, hierarchical, formal accountability for institutional activity. From this perspective, loosely coupled organizations are loosely coupled on those action dimensions that are of no direct external concern. This is not to say the larger environment does not pay a price for lack of concern with the action dimensions on which educational organizations remain loosely coupled. It is simply an assertion that loose coupling need not necessarily—and, in the case of educational organizations, does not actually—spread to all levels of organizational activity.

On the contrary, as Meyer and Rowan (1983) argue, what remains loosely coupled is the dimension of action that falls below environmental salience in analyzing the organizations in question. Functional domains highly salient to the external environment come under the control of centralized, formal administration. In effect, it would appear, "what counts out there" is (rightly or not) not left to loose linkage arrangements. For sensible or not so sensible reasons, it gets "organized" and "controlled." In effect, "the iron law of oligarchy" lives—at the strategic level. Fortunately, some oligarchies are more open than others. Certainly, the executive level of a university can easily function as one of the most open of all. The analysis would suggest that the reason for this is not conspicuous egalitarianism, but the very necessity of building strategic coherence atop loose linkage. The leadership envisioned is an exercise in fluid mechanics, not soil engineering.

Meyer and Rowen (1983) write:

> Consider this matter from the viewpoint of any rational college president or school superintendent. The whole school will dissolve in conflict and illegitimacy if the internal and external understanding of its accredited status is in doubt. (pp. 84–85) . . . The system of inspection and control [is] formulated to avoid inspecting the actual instructional activities and outcomes of schooling. That is, a school's formal structure (its ritual classifications) is "decoupled" from technical activities and outcomes. (pp. 87–88) The classifications of education, however, are not rules to be cynically manipulated. They are the sacred rituals that give meaning to the whole enterprise, both internally and externally. These categories are understood everywhere to *index* education. They are not understood to

be education, but they are also not understood simply to be alienating bureaucratic constraints. So the decoupling that is characteristic of school systems must be carried out by all participants in the utmost good faith. Interaction in school systems, therefore, is characterized both by the assumption of good faith and the actualities of decoupling. This is *the logic of confidence*: Parties bring to each other the taken-for-granted, good-faith assumption that the other is, in fact, carrying out his or her defined activity. (p. 90)

The concept of a "logic of confidence" raises the issue of how loosely linked organizations like mega-universities can "gear up" to move to the "warp-speed" dimension of HRO-like performance. How do organizations with such loose linkages develop high-reliability capability, and what can be inferred about the nature of the leadership that institutional executives with a strategic agenda and institution-wide concerns will need to exhibit? In the remainder of this chapter I will suggest that the leadership approach required is not the leadership approach formerly recommended for universities seen as loosely linked institutions. I will explain why the continuing education function and a variety of available continuing education structures constitute extremely powerful tools for the executive leadership of the mega-university.

STRATEGIC LEADERSHIP FOR LOOSELY COUPLED INSTITUTIONS

In their landmark study of the American college presidency, sponsored by the Carnegie Commission on Higher Education, Cohen and March (1974/1986) set the strategic mission of the presidency in the context of a loosely coupled organizational system immersed in ambiguity. This study is a richly imaginative and creative work, a classic valued as much for its contribution to organization theory as for its substantive analysis of the college president's function in American higher education. However, for my purposes I will confine discussion of Cohen and March to a single issue: the applicability of their recommendations for leadership strategies to the challenge of the coming wave. In that regard, it seems fair to say that the recommendations stemming from their observations prior to 1974 are inadequate to the new demands. The nature of the inadequacy reveals the special character of the new pressures.

In hindsight, the leadership orientation recommended by Cohen and March can be seen to fit calmer institutional times — notwithstanding the heated political rhetoric of that era. Their prescriptions for presidential behavior focused on maintaining what might be called "becalmed effectiveness at the margins of the doable." This domain did not seem to cover a very large area even then.

Thus, for example, the enlightened college president was advised to spend more time on decisionmaking than did others in the system in order to wear them out, given the universally low time investment in decisionmaking. Similarly, the executive was advised to persist, because what had been rejected in the past might well be accepted by a new set of actors with no institutional memory, and because things decided do not automatically transpire unless they are continually nudged along.

Somewhat more calculatingly, the college president was advised to overload the system in order to compel action, drive away opponents with little energy, and thereby keep so many irons in the fire that there would be no need to remain committed to a particular one. Instead there would arise a measure of flexibility and safety against contingencies: if one project did not bear fruit, another would.

In a similar vein, the authors encouraged providing "garbage cans" for decisionmaking. This meant the creation of highly symbolic, empty events, whereby the distracting power of status concerns and rhetoric could be drained away from the real agendas and from actors with real power who desired to get things done. College presidents were also advised to "manage unobtrusively" — in effect, to lower their public action profiles, to leverage their own system with carefully chosen acts at the margins of issues that could have significant long-term effects, and to use the power of bureaucratic action — "signing a piece of paper" — to create an institutional status quo which an opponent would be hard put to alter.

Cohen and March's (1974/1986) final rule for the shrewd college president of the early 1970s was to "interpret history" — before others would, in effect. The system was presumed to be one of such low salience and interest, with such ambiguous connections between what transpired, what was thought to have transpired, and what was thought to account for what had transpired, that an actor with an agenda would be free to find precedent for it in the fog that passed for institutional experience. One or two other consensus-broadening tactical rules were suggested as well. It is somewhat disturbing that the list was not altered in the second edition (Cohen & March, 1986, pp. 207–215).

Machiavellian tactics notwithstanding, the significant point for us is that the strategic agenda implied by the preceding list appears more quaint than cynical. It is no longer satisfactory merely to have eluded windbags or fed the status-hungry within the confines of the institution. It is now necessary to address significant environmental needs — and sometimes actual demands — for new university roles and capabilities. A fuzzy institutional memory is not an asset. History cannot now be creatively interpreted without the consent of external parties, and that consent is not likely to materialize. The system is hardly in need of artificial overloading; it is more likely in danger of being genuinely overwhelmed. Worse, the creation of empty, symbolic events and issues for allegedly harmless venting runs the serious risk of perpetuating institutional immaturity. When external challenges arrive, the articulate immature may be safely distracted, but this will not produce the needed numbers of serious and ready respondents.

Similarly, persistence is a trait relevant to a trial-and-error-oriented organization. It is not relevant to an environment that is fast-paced and unforgiving, and does not offer second chances. Managing unobtrusively is likewise inadequate to occasions when decisiveness and the courage and knowledge to lead in an explicit, public commitment are required by the actors and, more importantly, the dynamics of the external environment.

In effect, the leadership skills now required of the executive level of mega-universities are skills appropriate to leading HROs — but HROs with loosely linked internal operations, with high ritual significance in society, and with the need for crisply executed acts on behalf of the whole toward the external environment (Ellis, 1991; McCall, 1981; Conger et al., 1988; Lerner & Wanat, 1992). The combination that is required is *strategically informed flexibility*. The value of continuing education — as a function and as a variety of available structures — should become clear in the following discussion of strategically informed flexibility.

DURABILITY AND HIGH PERFORMANCE: THE ELEMENTS OF STRATEGICALLY INFORMED FLEXIBILITY

Landau (1991) has argued that multiorganizational systems in which the component organizations are loosely linked offer high system reliability because component organizations with overlapping capabilities can serve in place of one another. Such a system has the reliability of a market: the system continues to perform even as individual participants increase or decrease in effectiveness. The whole is more reliable than the sum of the parts.

Reliability is especially valuable where system errors would be very hazardous. Overlap among component units in an organization — or component organizations in a multiorganizational system — constitutes flexibility, and flexibility is a key adaptive capability because one can never predict when or how a component will fail, or (usually) why. This view of flexibility as a prime adaptive capacity is shared by those concerned with long-term reliability.

Others are concerned with reliability in the face of high performance pressure, often in an explosive, short time frame. These two interests in reliability amount to relative emphases on durability and precision. Precision performance (maintained through continuous situational assessment by expert teams) seems to be the issue in HROs of LaPorte and Consolini's description. Durability seems to be the issue in loosely linked, market-like structures, such as urban transportation systems, of the type discussed by Landau. There durability appears to derive from mixed cooperative-competitive interests in stabilizing the multi-actor relationship.

The mega-university will increasingly need both durability and precision performance capabilities of a higher order than was required in the past. Where an institution is loosely linked, in its internal academic activities, it needs *durability*. In the face of changing student needs and expectations, changing faculty profiles and interests, changing competitors, and changing organizational clients, it must continuously adjust its overlaps and mixes of offerings, structures, formats, and activities; it must admit, teach, graduate, research, capture grants, invest, solicit funds, publish, hire, promote, fire, staff, house, financially assist, deliver workshops, host meetings, and so on, through its latticework of internal, semi-independent entities.

In carrying out more or less familiar activities, mixed competitive-cooperative interests, low external regulation, and the overlapping interests and capabilities of a variety of units assure creative solutions. On this dimension, executive leadership can pick and/or let emerge capable units for a variety of challenges—problems or opportunities stimulated by external events, but manifested as internally initiated adjustments.

Sometimes, however, the external environment articulates a specific, system-level demand (opportunity or problem), or the leadership of an institution wishes to initiate an institutional-level venture in that rapidly moving environment—to reposition itself with respect to a situation which it wishes to shape rather than simply adjust to. In such cases the institution must exhibit *precision performance*.

Working with internal faculty and administrative experts, the executive level must decide whether to go forward with a program, resources, and institutional commitment (Lerner, 1976a; Lerner, 1976b; Thompson, 1977). This is no time for a market. Instead, an ad hoc decision team operating under the banner of formal organizational authority, combining faculty experts and executive staff, is required in support of senior executive initiatives.

Thus, the mega-university of the future needs both hands-off and hands-on leadership from the executive level, depending on the nature of the problem or opportunity. If the problem is subsystemic, the executive should stand back; if it is suprasystemic, the executive should lead aggressively, albeit with the aid of an appropriate expert cadre suitable to the issue (Katz & Kahn, 1978).

Enter Continuing Education as Tool and Medium

The continuing education function and the variety of continuing education structures recognized in higher education can serve as valuable tools to university executives in these situations. They can be used for quick action at the supra-systemic, institutional level; they can also be used in maintaining continuous, reliable operations despite environmental changes. Continuing education is marvelously suited to serving both functions.

Continuing education as an administrative structure can be used to assemble groups of faculty from across departments, schools, and colleges, from other universities, and from nonacademic institutions employing researchers. For consulting, contract research, and instructional missions, continuing education centralizes and standardizes financial functions including, most importantly, accountability. It centralizes cross-unit communication and administrative support and services. Its use reduces fears that one participating unit will dominate in interunit ventures. It provides a vehicle for paying faculty and units for services and for distributing surplus revenues as the law, public and institutional rules, and extra-institutional restrictions may allow. Thus it avoids competing with vested interests when fashioning new interests.

Several continuing education structures can serve this purpose. (The various structures are discussed more fully in Chapter 5.) Continuing education structures become a focus for leading and organizing what would otherwise be a series of ad hoc contacts among potential collaborators. A centralized continuing education unit can identify necessary or interested parties who may be psychologically or culturally distant from some of the participants who initiated discussions. Also, the continuing education office is a potential venture capitalist, financier, and banker on behalf of participating units. It has the capacity to develop programs, remunerate faculty, distribute developmental funds to instructional units, and organize interunit proposals to an external market. Informality, a relatively loose structure, an atmosphere promoting discussion among relevant parties, facilitation, and tactful mediation—all these are among the capabilities of an effective continuing education office. Such an office can assemble teams and "deals" to make proposed new programs a reality.

Furthermore, unit interests in given interunit programs, and whole programs, can be truncated or even aborted far more easily under continuing education arrangements for funding, staffing, and delivery than in departmental structures. Conventional units resist program termination. However, the changing environment represented by the coming wave requires flexibility; an institution must differentiate between a timely idea and one that is premature or obsolete.

For example, a continuing education unit can offset the termination of a "zoology in primary education program" offered to zoos with the debut of a "music and geriatric studies program" developed with and for a consortium of nursing homes. Inflexible persistence for purposes of bureaucratic self-protection is less likely to occur in a centralized continuing education unit than if individual academic units are relied on to fill a programming need. I do not advocate obstructing unit creativity, but coordinating university undertakings so as to protect the strategic profile of the whole.

At the national level, when things work the way they should, the chief executive identifies an environmental challenge (a need and/or opportunity); declares an institutional commitment—in effect, a mission; seeks the internal articulation of program components for that mission; and then re-presents those components, under the banner of that mission, to that environment, becoming an actor in that environment, having brought that environment into the organization, as it were, to assess how best to operationalize the desire to act upon that environment. (Lately presidents have shown a tendency to stop after the "mission articulation" stage—which itself can be more or less fully developed, ranging from incomplete sentences at a regular news conference to what used to be called a domestic policy.)

The process should not be different in the mega-university. When the executive leadership of the institution has identified an opportunity in the environment, or has articulated a broad mission, an internal process should be triggered to gather and order operational components on behalf of this institution-wide, supra-systemic venture.

In some institutions the internal elements are well articulated beforehand and "merely" need marshaling. Alternatively, the declaration of mission may be intended to serve—or, alas, had better now serve—as the impetus for developing competitive operational capabilities in support.

Whether the goal is to round up existing forces in the service of an effort featuring the whole more than the parts, or to aid the rapid equipping and coordination of skeletal components for a new institutional priority, continuing education is an attractive operating dimension for senior administration.

As less than a line unit of a given line college, there is less inertia to overcome in starting program ventures through continuing education compared to what executive leaders must often negotiate with line colleges. Similarly, closing down programs that have outlived or never demonstrated their usefulness is a simpler affair through continuing education. This is a major asset to an institution seeking to reduce the costs of proactivity as much as possible.

Depending on the continuing education unit's mode of financing (see Chapter 6) and its structural format and mission priority (see Chapter 5), continuing education can be a useful source of funding, and particularly a seed-money source, given its continuously changing financial base.

A properly staffed continuing education unit—particularly one that uses faculty consultants for program development—can be a useful liaison between executive administration and specialized sectors of the external environment. This role is discussed more fully in Chapter 7.

The discussion of structuring continuing education that is outlined in this chapter and developed in several later chapters stops short of taking elaboration to its outer limit: the creation of yet another college in the mega-university. A College of Continuing Education, or a School of General Studies, raises the question of whether the benefits inherent in a flexible, swiftly reacting, cost-effective staff unit can be retained if it is made into a major division of the institution. My view is that, ultimately, the responsiveness to mission and the capacity for flexibility that such a College of Continuing Education or School of General Studies can offer will depend on three factors: (1) the stability of the market supporting such an entity with students, relationships with interested nonacademic institutions, adjunct faculty, and research and co-development opportunities; (2) the leadership skills at the executive level of the mega-university; and (3) whether the university has the maturity required to maintain a healthy relationship between conventional line colleges and a college of continuing education.

By "maturity" I do not mean the psychosocial level of behavior, which leadership can help to develop over a reasonable period. Rather, I mean the state of curriculum, research, and development plans that conventional colleges have attained. When these are not sufficiently matured, tensions with a full-blown College of Continuing Education or School of General Studies can persist at harmful levels. Line colleges that are not sure what they are seeking or how to go about it cannot be counted on to understand a subtle set of constructively overlapping relationships supporting complementary priorities.

REFERENCES

Cohen, M., & March, J. (1986). *Leadership and ambiguity* (2nd ed.). Cambridge, MA: Harvard Business School Press (1st edition published 1974).

Conger, J. A., Kanungo, R. N., et al. (1988). *Charismatic leadership: The elusive factor in organizational leadership.* San Francisco: Jossey-Bass.

Ellis, R. J. (1991). Explaining the occurrence of charismatic leadership in organizations. *Journal of Theoretical Politics, 3*(3), 305–320.

Katz, D., & Kahn, R. L. (1978). *The social psychology of organizations* (2nd ed.). New York: Wiley.

Landau, M. (1969). Redundancy, rationality and the problem of duplication and overlap. *Public Administration Review, 39*(6), 346–358.

Landau, M. (1973). On the concept of self-correcting organization. *Public Administration Review, 43*(6), 533–539.

Landau, M. (1991). On multiorganizational systems in public administration. *Journal of Public Administration Research and Theory, 1*(1), 5–18.

LaPorte, T., & Consolini, P. (1991). Working in practice but not in theory: Theoretical challenges of "high-reliability organizations." *Journal of Public Administration Research and Theory, 1*(1), 19–47.

Lerner, A. (1976a). *The politics of decision making.* Beverly Hills, CA: Sage.

Lerner, A. (1976b). *Experts, politicians, and decisionmaking in the technological society.* Morristown, NJ: General Learning Press.

Lerner, A. (1986). There is more than one way to be redundant: A comparison of alternatives for the design and use of redundancy in organizations. *Administration and Society, 18*(3), 334–359.

Lerner, A., & Wanat, J. (1992). *Public administration: A realistic reinterpretation of contemporary public management.* Englewood Cliffs, NJ: Prentice-Hall.

Lustick, I. (1980). Explaining the variable utility of disjointed incrementalism. *American Political Science Review, 74*(2), 342–353.

Lynton, E. A., & Elman, S. E. (1987). *New priorities for the University.* San Francisco: Jossey-Bass.

March, J., & Olsen, J. (1976). *Ambiguity and choice in organizations.* Bergen, Norway: Universitetsforlaget.

Matejko, A. (1986). *The self-defeating organization.* New York: Praeger.

McCall, M. (1981). *Leadership and the professional: report No. 17.* Greensboro, N.C.: Center for Creative Leadership.

Meyer, J., & Rowan, B. (1983). The structure of educational organizations. In J. Meyer & R. Scott, *Organizational environments* (pp. 71–98). Beverly Hills, CA: Sage.

Ott, J. (1989). *The organizational culture perspective.* Pacific Grove, CA: Brooks/Cole.

Perrow, C. (1984). *Normal accidents.* New York: Basic Books.

Peters, T., & Waterman, R. (1982). *In search of excellence.* New York: Warner.

Scott, W., & Hart, D. (1989). *Organizational values.* New Brunswick, NJ: Transaction.

Thompson, V. (1977). *Modern organizations* (2nd ed.). University, AL: University of Alabama.

Weick, K. (1976). Educational organizations as loosely coupled systems. *Administrative Science Quarterly, 21*, 1–19.

Weick, K. (1979). *The social psychology of organizing* (2nd ed.). Reading, MA: Addison-Wesley.

Woodhouse, E. (1988). Sophisticated trial and error in decision making about risk. In M. Kraft, & N. Vig, *Technology and Politics* (pp. 208–226). Durham, NC: Duke University Press.

2

Population Diversity and the Organization and Function of Continuing Higher Education

Joe F. Donaldson
Jovita M. Ross-Gordon

The next several years will witness profound changes within our society's population. America will continue to age, will become increasingly diverse, and will grow more dependent upon a work force that differs from the work force of the past. These changes have important implications for continuing higher education and will create opportunities for leadership, opportunities the likes of which have seldom if ever been available. Continuing educators must understand the nature of these changes and be willing to explore new ways of thinking about their work in order to take advantage of these opportunities and to effectively meet the challenges they present. This chapter discusses how such understanding and new ways of thinking might be achieved.

In the first part of the chapter we consider population changes and their implications for continuing higher education. We address enrollment trends in higher education; review demographic trends, enrollment trends in general, and the enrollment patterns of diverse groups; detail coming changes in America's work force; and provide examples of continuing education's programmatic responses to these changes. In the second part of the chapter, we turn our attention to the question of how continuing education can organize itself to respond effectively to the environmental turbulence and heterogeneity created by these very changes. We argue that a key to success will be continuing education's ability to develop an organizational capacity for learning that bridges the many cultures with which it will work both within and outside the university.

POPULATION CHANGES: IMPLICATIONS FOR CONTINUING EDUCATION

Enrollment Trends in Higher Education

The traditional student in higher education becomes an increasing rarity as more and more students manifest one or more nontraditional characteristics. Students age 25 or older have become commonplace, representing 39% of the college student population in 1988 (Baker & Thompson, 1989). It has been forecast that by the year 2000, 50% of higher education students will be over age 25, with 20% being age 35 or older (American Association of State Colleges and Universities & National Association of State Universities and Land Grant Colleges, 1986). The past 10 years have witnessed an approximately 45% increase in the number of higher education students between the ages of 35 and 44 (National Center for Educational Statistics, 1988).

Associated with the growth of the adult student population is the growing predominance of part-time attendance, which has risen 109% over the last 20 years ("Part-time Higher," 1990). Part-time students now outnumber those attending full-time 3 : 1 in two-year public institutions and constitute approximately 31% of students in four-year public institutions. This trend is expected to continue into the 1990s, although the rate of increase is expected to diminish ("Part-time enrollments," 1990).

Women, more than men, have contributed to the dramatic increase in college enrollment by adults over the last several decades. Women over 35 attended college during 1988 at a rate nearly twice that of men in the same age group (Bruno, 1990). Women's participation exceeds that of men across racial ethnic groups, although the gap is most pronounced for Blacks and whites. This increase in the proportion of female college students from 41% of the college population in 1970 to 54% in 1988 can be largely attributed to the continuing attendance of "older" women (Baker & Thompson, 1989). Women over 25 constitute 42.2% of female college students while men over 25 account for only 35.6% of the male student group. Women are more likely to attend part-time than men, thus accounting for a large part of the growth in part-time enrollment.

The growth in part-time attendance is largely attributed to the rising number of adult students, but Aslanian (1990) notes that more and more younger students "act like older students"; they may commute to school; attend part-time, evenings, or week-ends; or attend several colleges, serially. Carroll (1989), reporting on findings of an analysis of follow-up data from respondents to the 1980 High School and Beyond project, concludes: "There is a substantial body of evidence that the traditional persistence track is not the track followed by a majority of students who earn bachelor's degrees" (p. 9). The traditional student he refers to is one who goes on to college directly after high school, enrolls in a four-year institution for the first year, proceeds to complete the second semester immediately after the first, and then continues on to graduation. It is noted that while males were more likely than females not to enroll in college at all during the first five years after high school, females were more likely to start off track — by delaying attendance, attending part-time, or beginning at a two-year institution.

Adults are not only returning to college to earn undergraduate degrees. They are also returning in increasing numbers to attend graduate school part-time after being in the world of work. In 1986–87 part-time graduate enrollments accounted for about 54% of the total graduate enrollments in American colleges (National Center for Education Statistics, 1986; "Part-time Students Account," 1988). More and more graduate students are inter-mixing work and study, especially in professional schools, rather than continuing directly to graduate study from their undergraduate experiences. More than half of graduate students are 30 years or older ("Part-time students, 1988).

The need to maintain and develop a competent work force, the mandate of many states that professionals continue their education, and the zest for learning among an increasing number of the adult population have also contributed to a growth in the number of noncredit programs and of students enrolling in them. In short, continuing higher education is one of the fastest-growing components of higher education.

Demographic Trends/Enrollment Trends for Diverse Groups

This new wave of adult learners, brought on by (a) a surge in the adult population that will continue into the twenty-first century and (b) our society's increasing focus on economic development, international competition, and the need for skilled and knowledgeable workers, creates many opportunities, challenges, and questions for continuing education. This new wave of learners, however, masks an undertow of other demographic changes that raises serious issues for continuing education in particular and higher education more generally. As Briscoe and Ross (1989) note, America is not only graying, "the skin color of America is also changing and in a way that cannot continue to be ignored" (p. 584).

Immigration, higher birth rates, and concentration of the population at younger age levels have all contributed to growth in the proportion of the population that might be labeled as "minority." The Asian population grew by 70% between 1980 and 1988, with Hispanics as the next fastest-growing segment of the U.S. population, at a growth rate of 34% ("The Asian Population," 1990). Less remarkable growth rates were reported for Native Americans than for whites (6%). Comparable increases in the participation rates of minority adults in adult education in general and continuing higher education in particular have not been observed, to the extent that current data collection patterns even permit such observations. The most recent data from the National Center of Education Statistics indicate that 8.1% of Blacks, 8.2% of Hispanics, and 14.5% of whites participated in some form of adult education in 1984 (Snyder, 1988). In the same year Black adults represented 6% of adult education participants (down from 7% 15 years earlier) while comprising 11% of the general population (up from 10% 15 years earlier) (Hill, 1987). O'Brien (1990) reports figures from a 1985 College Board survey of students age 25 or older enrolled in credit programs. Data from that study reflect participation patterns as follows: 88% white, 7% Black, 2% Hispanic, and .4% other. It seems clear that adult and continuing higher education have not kept pace in serving the rising proportion of the "minority" population.

This chapter focuses particularly on those "minority" groups that appear to be underrepresented in adult and higher education. Asians present a unique case in that rarely are they considered educationally underrepresented. Carroll (1989) notes that Asians were 14% more likely than whites to embark on the persistence track (starting college immediately after high school, at a four-year institution, and continuing without interruption through graduation. In 1986 Asians represented 3.6% of undergraduate and 16.2% of graduate enrollments, although they account for only 2.7% of the population (Wilson & Carter, 1988; "The Asian Population," 1990).

Asian students' disproportionately high representation in higher education does not, in a democratic society such as our own, warrant the quotas that some institutions are said to have instituted to cap Asian enrollment. At the same time, there does not, at first glance, seem to be an urgent need for programs aimed at increasing Asian enrollment in higher education. Future data collection within adult education and closer examination of patterns of participation by the "other" category may reveal particular areas of continuing education where Asians have not had proportional participation. Meanwhile programs aimed at improving intercultural communications and understanding will still need to consider all segments of the U.S. population, whether educationally underrepresented or not.

Is there a pool of potential students?   Some might argue that since there is a close correlation between a population segment's education and income levels and its participation in adult education (broadly defined), failure to complete high school explains why some minority groups are less likely to participate in adult and higher education. Yet, despite well-publicized high rates of high school noncompletion among minorities in many urban areas, their overall level of educational attainment has risen steadily in recent decades. Between 1970 and 1987, Blacks and Hispanics nearly closed the almost three-year gap that had existed between Blacks/Hispanic levels of educational attainment and that of whites. Now median educational attainment levels for all three groups fall in the 12th year (U.S. Bureau of the Census, 1989). A gap persists, however, between the college enrollment rates of "traditional-age" white students and students from Black/Hispanic backgrounds. Whites still outdistance the other groups, with 39% of whites going on to college in the 1988 school year, while only 28% of Blacks and 31% of Hispanics pursued a higher education directly after high school (Bruno, 1990).

Minority college attendance peaked in 1976 with 33% of those who completed high school attending college among Blacks and 36% among Hispanics (Wilson & Carter, 1988). More recent reports show surges in college attendance that are inconsistent across minority groups. In 1988 Asian enrollment showed an annual growth rate of 111% compared to 7.2% for Blacks. Several sources have indicated a need for particular concern over declining enrollments among African-American males (Magner, 1990; Wilson & Carter, 1988). With rising educational attainment through the high school level, persistent gaps in traditional-age college enrollment, and nearly twice as many whites over 25 holding a college degree as Blacks and Hispanics (Kominski, 1988; U.S. Bureau of the Census, 1989) it appears that there is a large pool of potential continuing higher education students among Blacks and Hispanics. It is also true that among Blacks and Hispanics who are enrolled in college the proportion of students over age 25 has been very similar to that of whites (Bruno, 1990), despite the fact that a smaller proportion of older minority individuals than older whites have completed high school (U.S. Bureau of the Census, 1989). This suggests that these individuals are in fact quite recruitable to higher education.

Enrollment patterns. As we work to improve the participation of minority individuals in continuing higher education, we need to examine their patterns of enrollment by institutional type. Enrollment data from as recently as 1988 indicate that among students 35 and older Hispanics are overrepresented at two-year institutions and underrepresented at four-year colleges and in graduate programs (Bruno, 1990). Blacks in that age range are overrepresented in two-year programs, proportionately represented at four-year colleges, and underrepresented in graduate education. For many minority adults a two-year institution may be the most appropriate choice, particularly if they are interested in the numerous career options available to holders of a specialized associate-level degree. For students, however, whose ultimate goal is completion of a four-year degree program and who have chosen a two-year institution because it is financially and geographically more accessible, the transition to a four-year institution may be more complicated than they anticipate. Although his data are based on analysis of traditional-age students in the High School and Beyond database, Carroll (1989) found that students who began college "off track" (after a delay, at a less-than-a-four-year institution, or part-time) were one-fifth as likely as others to complete a bachelor's degree during the five years studied. While this study did not examine the entire pool of adult students, some of its findings are nonetheless interesting. Carroll reports that

1. Proportionately more Hispanics began in two-year institutions;
2. Twenty-eight percent of all 1980 graduates who left the persistence track (took time off, changed to part-time, or transferred to a two-year institution) graduated; in this category only 14% of Blacks and 16% of Hispanics graduated;
3. Blacks were more likely than whites or Hispanics to drop out;
4. Low-socioeconomic-status (low-SES) students were three times as likely to drop out as high-SES students;
5. Socioeconomic status was highly related to the type of start and to persistence; and
6. More than five of every six 1980 high school graduates did not enter college or did not persevere in the traditional fashion. That is, only 157 of every 1,000 students earned a bachelor's degree in four years.

While no data were located on the persistence rates of minority adults, these data suggest that not only ethnicity but also institutional type, SES, and part-time status all influence persistence rates and need to be assessed as variables that may affect the persistence of non-traditional-age students.

A Changing Work Force

The existence of a large pool of minority adults who have not participated in higher education at levels equivalent to those of the white majority has great significance for society and higher education. Analysts looking at the changing face of the American workplace have emphasized the declining presence of the white male as increasing proportions of workers are female, U.S.-born representatives of ethnic minority groups, or immigrants (National Alliance of Business, 1986; Nussbaum, 1988). White U.S.-born males composed 47% of the work force in 1985; they are expected to represent only 15% of new entrants into the labor force between 1985 and 2000 (Nussbaum, 1988). Without a significant increase in their college participation rates or adult education experiences to provide further education, many from this growing minority segment of the work force will find themselves relegated to low-level service occupations. The disappearance of the industrial economy and its replacement by a technology-based information economy may have a major impact on the economic status of minority workers. While African-Americans and Hispanics are proportionately represented or overrepresented in a number of rapidly growing occupational areas such as cooks, guards, health aides, and computer operators, they are underrepresented in more financially lucrative and high-skill growth occupations such as managers and executives, registered nurses, computer systems analysts, computer programmers, and electronics engineers (U.S. Bureau of the Census, 1989).

Business and industry provided nearly as many courses to adults in 1984 (6,850,000) as did four-year colleges and universities (6,900,000) (Hill, 1987). However, continuing higher education is still uniquely qualified to provide leadership in training minority adults in the emerging and expanding occupations. Hodgkinson (1985) notes that fewer and fewer opportunities exist for individuals to move up within organizations without the kind of educational preparation needed to secure professional and managerial jobs. In a kind of Catch-22, professional-technical staff and managers are three times as likely to receive employer-provided training as are workers at lower occupational levels (Zemsky, 1983). Zemsky, basing his examination on patterns of employer-provided and -sponsored training as reported through the triennial survey of adult education over the period 1969-81, notes that "even when education and age were taken into account, nonwhites, particularly those with minimal levels of schooling, received significantly less training than similarly schooled whites in the same age group" (p. 8). As late as 1987 a similar picture prevailed. At that time African-American adults constituted 9.5% of the work force and Hispanics 5.5%. However, they received respectively only 5.1 and 2.7% of the formal workplace training (Carnevale, 1989). Whites, who constituted 86% of the work force, received 92.2% of workplace training. On the other hand, nonwhites were more likely than whites to have participated in employer-sponsored education and training, much of which is provided by two-year and four-year colleges. These data suggest the critical role that continuing higher education has to play in this area.

This role is further emphasized by evidence that both Blacks and women gain a greater earnings advantage through completion of a college degree than do whites or men (Baker & Thompson, 1989). The earnings ratio (improvement in earnings as further education is completed) is not as dramatically affected by completion of one to three years of college, although this amount of education does yield earnings ratios comparable to those of men and whites. Unfortunately, similar earnings returns after participation in higher education do not offset the difference in base income apparent after high school completion: Blacks who have completed high school earn 79% as much as their white counterparts, and women earn 64% as much as men.

In addition to improving educational and employment opportunities for minority adults, continuing higher education can play an important role in the changing American workplace through the development of cross-cultural training programs for managers and staff. Copeland (1988) and others agree with John Naisbitt's contention that the big challenge of the 1980s is not the retraining of workers but the retraining of managers. Copeland suggests that organizations seeking the most productive employees will have to "compete for women, minorities and others who are different from the norm in age, appearance, physical ability and lifestyle," and adds that "they will also have to develop and retrain them" (p. 49). This goal can be facilitated by two means: (a) increasing diversity at the higher levels of the organization, and (b) working with managers and other employees to develop an organizational climate that not only tolerates but appreciates the diversity of perspectives brought by a "new" work force. In the past, employers could forestall race-related interpersonal conflicts by segregating employees into racially and culturally uniform work groups. Organizational changes, advanced technology, and an emphasis on quality improvement will require that individuals be prepared to work in flexible and frequently reconstructed work groups or task forces that will place greater demands on cross-cultural communication and interpersonal skills (Goddard, 1989).

Women are a growing presence in the workplace and are expected to constitute as much as 42% of the new work force between 1985 and 2000 (Nussbaum, 1988). Many current organizational policies regarding pay, fringe benefits, time away from work, pensions, welfare, and other issues were designed for a society in which men worked and women stayed home (Goddard, 1989). Obvious implications of women's entry into the work force are increasing demands for day care, time off for family leave and emergencies, and flexible and stay-at-home jobs (Goddard, 1989). Less obvious is the need to design training and career development programs that acknowledge the special barriers women may face in the workplace, including barriers to participation in such programs. Equally important are programs that prepare managers to mentor women to take on leadership positions and that prepare workers and managers to accept the wider range of leadership styles that women may incorporate into the work environment.

These changes in the workplace and the work force will require extensive educational activity. Already many organizations are designing programs that respond to such needs. Xerox Corporation has long been active in this arena, and its "Balanced Workforce Strategy" has led to demonstrable success in facilitating upward mobility for women and minorities, doubling the representation of women and nearly doubling the representation of minorities in managerial ranks between 1978 and 1988 (Solomon, 1989). Solomon describes numerous similar efforts by other companies including Digital, Hewlett-Packard, Honeywell, and Procter-Gamble, with successful programs often combining elements of individual development, management development, and organizational development. While these large corporations provide models for success, in coming years numerous smaller companies will look to outside providers, including the continuing education units of colleges and universities, for assistance in this area.

Recent Programmatic Efforts Within Continuing Higher Education

Aslanian (1990) speaks of several kinds of access that seem to be essential if adults are to function as an integrated part of higher education institutions. These forms of access include

1. Geographic access;
2. Logistical access;
3. Financial access;
4. Psychological access; and
5. Cultural access.

Existing programs for adult students address several of these issues of access. For instance, satellite campuses, off-campus programs, and downtown centers reflect institutional attempts to reduce the geographic barriers faced by adult students. Phone registration, extended hours for campus offices and services, and flexible course scheduling are ways of facilitating logistical access. Returning adult student centers, adult student organizations, and personnel designated to counsel adult students in academic and personal matters can all be seen as measures that affect psychological access. Yet rarely in the literature of continuing higher education do we see consideration given to dimensions of access as they particularly affect minority adults.

Kramer (1989) writes that failure to consider the needs of underrepresented groups is frequently based on erroneous assumptions, such as the myth that all African-American adults are educationally underprepared or cannot afford the fees associated with self-supporting continuing education programs. He commends campuses for recent efforts to reach out to high school and elementary school youth and create bridges to opportunities in higher education. Yet he laments that similar efforts have not been made to bring Black adults to campuses, where, he hypothesizes, their presence would enhance the environment for Black youth and create an institutional climate more receptive to diversity. His discussion leads us to a more in-depth examination of the numerous barriers to access, including psychological and cultural ones. Cain (1987) has discussed a number of psychological access issues that may differentially affect African-American reentry students, including lack of confidence, dealing with what he calls "malefic generosity" or paternalistic treatment, family-related problems, and conflict between long- and short-range goals. Henry (1985) also speaks of the feelings of isolation and lack of mentoring faced by minority women graduate students, who often are not aware of existing services for women.

In a recent issue of *Black Issues in Higher Education* several continuing education administrators discussed barriers they perceived as contributing to the underrepresentation of Black adults (O'Brien, 1990). Jeanette Taylor of the University of Cincinnati focused on psychological access barriers, noting that many African-American adults did not perceive their predominant white local institutions as places where they were welcome, based on past historical factors. Laura Myers of Clark College also highlighted this issue, but noted that student perceptions of institutions can change with time: "Some Hispanic students come in through the ESL programs on a part-time basis, and they get to the point where they feel comfortable walking around a college campus. Then they feel confident enough to start working on a degree" (O'Brien, 1990, p. 6). Psychological access seems to create more significant barriers for minority men, particularly among African-Americans, where similar patterns of a gender gap in representation have also been observed among traditional-age students. Likewise, financial access seems to pose a particular burden to many underrepresented adults, many of whom are not in a position to access employer support through tuition reimbursement (O'Brien, 1990). Jeanette Taylor urges institutions to revamp financial aid for part-time minority students. In her words: "We have to find a way to provide services for a population that cannot afford to pay as you go. It's a vicious cycle, because the ones who could gain the most from continuing education cannot afford it" (O'Brien, 1990, p. 6).

The Public Policy Program.   A number of programs have been created around the country that recognize the particular needs and concerns of students from underrepresented groups. One is the Public Policy Program originated at Saint Peter's College in Jersey City, New Jersey, during the mid-1970s to recruit, enroll, retain and graduate men and women residing in or near Jersey City (Surrey & Perry, 1986). Their mostly female (84%) participants have included teenage mothers, welfare recipients, single mothers, low-level public agency workers, teachers, and the un- and underemployed. During the most successful years of the program, 75% of the entering students completed the associate degree program and 50–60% of the associate degree graduates continued on to the bachelor of science degree. The authors identify increasing tuition rates, younger students, and students with poorer entry skills as possible reasons for a downward turn in retention in the mid-1980s. During that period only 40–50% of the students returned after the first year of instruction, a figure that many programs would find still impressive. The program's success has been attributed to its attention to the seven F's:

1. Finances;
2. Fatigue;
3. Flexibility;
4. Freedom;
5. Focus;
6. Friends; and
7. Future.

This list suggests that the Public Policy Program was designed to address all of the dimensions of access identified by Aslanian (1990) as posing potential barriers to adults.

The University Preparation Program. Beaty and Chiste (1986) describe a six-week University Preparation Program (UPP) for Native American students at the University of Lethbridge, Alberta, Canada, where the majority of Native American students are said to be re-entry students. The program was seen as a first step toward preparing Native Americans as teachers. Designers of the program were particularly cognizant of the difficulties many Native American students experience when they enter an academic setting where a different world view prevails, and face social isolation and misunderstanding. The issue of cultural access is addressed in the opening unit, which covers Native American history. This part of the curriculum reflects an attempt to build student self-esteem, establish group bonding, and enable students to identify values they wish to retain. Classroom techniques used in the program are said to be drawn from the areas of adult education, counseling group work, business management, community development, and international education, with an aim of fostering self-directed learners who will also be able to cope with traditional didactic college classrooms. The authors' assessment of the program reports not only the quantitative successes—program completion rates of 57% and 70% in the first two years, with 41% and 43% respectively continuing on to complete their first year of the college—but also the qualitative judgment that some who did not return nonetheless experienced significant personal development, which in some cases influenced students' subsequent choices. Beaty and Chiste question whether universities, in requiring Native Americans (and we can include here other cultural groups) to abandon traditional views, do not risk depriving students of the self-esteem that is necessary for effective learning.

The Minority Continuing Education Opportunities Program. A program that has won a creative programming award and served as a model for a number of university continuing education programs is the Minority Continuing Education Opportunities Program (MCEOP) at Ohio State University (Kramer, 1989; Moe, 1989). MCEOP, developed specifically to attract minority adults to undergraduate and graduate programs of the university, involves an alliance among the university, local corporations and businesses, and individual students. According to Kramer,

> Corporate recommendations rather than test scores or prior education records are employed to identify prospective students. The program admits students whose potential for and interest in learning has been documented in the workplace and whose career circumstances may be enhanced as a consequence of university enrollment. (1989, p. 4)

Once admitted, students are provided an array of support services, including individualized academic counseling and group advisement sessions (on nonacademic procedural topics or social events) designed to foster the development of a peer-support group. Critical to the success of the program is a recyclable tuition program, through which money for paying tuition for initial courses is combined in a pool so that future employer tuition "reimbursements" can be used to pay for courses at the time of registration rather than at completion. As students complete or leave the program, they or their employers replenish the tuition pool with the amount of the initial course investment. Consequently, students are never faced with the financial burden of paying for courses prior to enrollment and waiting for reimbursement at the end. This program addresses both financial and psychological access barriers that have previously discouraged minority adults from enrolling in continuing higher education programs. On this program's value to the institution, Kramer adds that the program has altered the composition of the black student body in a way in which black students of all ages can more meaningfully, immediately, and directly impact upon the development of an institutional environment which celebrates diversity as an essential and dynamic institutional characteristic. (p. 4)

Other programs. In addition to the programs reported here as serving minority adults as individuals, a number of continuing education programs have become involved in more comprehensive efforts aimed at changing the nature of the curriculum and organizational culture to more effectively serve minority adults. A recent newsletter of the National University Continuing Education Association (NUCEA) ("Continuing Education," 1990–1991) describes a few such programs. For instance, at the University of Minnesota, Continuing Education and Extension has integrated courses that explore the diversity of culture into its regular curriculum as part of its "Compleat Scholar" program. Course titles such as "The Making of the American People: Historical Roots of Cultural Differences" reveal an intent to incorporate information on diverse groups into existing courses rather than isolating that content into special topics courses. At Ohio State University brown-bag lunches that feature discussion on various diversity issues including minority concerns, women's issues, and gay and lesbian concerns have been planned to promote awareness among the continuing education staff. A broad systems approach is evidenced in the recommendations of the UNEX Plan to Enhance Cultural Diversity developed by Extension's Committee on Cultural Diversity at the University of California-Irvine. Recommendations include (a) making efforts to ensure that the applicant pool for new extension positions is culturally mixed, (b) adding a module on cultural diversity to every certificate program, and (c) developing a staff development notebook containing handouts on cultural diversity to which staff members are encouraged to make additional contributions.

The program issues and descriptions presented here provide only a partial perspective on an area in which developments are emerging even as we go to press and which has only recently started to be addressed in conference agendas and continuing higher education journals. The issues of access raised here will require our continued attention as we plan programs meant to broaden our base of service to previously underrepresented groups. The programs described here are in the vanguard in developing approaches to changing the structures and processes of continuing higher education as they interact with potential students, business and industry, and local community groups.

NEW APPROACHES IN STRUCTURE AND PROCESSES

How can continuing higher education respond to the changes just described and the issues identified? One possible approach takes advantage of organizational theory, particularly that branch dealing with organizational learning. Three major and interrelated theses will be developed as part of the analysis that follows:

1. Because it operates at the boundary of the institution, continuing education is in a unique position to assist universities in responding to these changes, but only if it develops its boundary-spanning capacity more fully.
2. The continuing education unit must be organized and administered so that its structure and function can evolve hand in hand with changing circumstances. Such evolution will be required in order to deal effectively with changes occurring in continuing education's environment.
3. The continuing education unit must be constituted and staffed so that the unit's capacity for cross-cultural organizational learning is nurtured and enhanced.

Spanning Boundaries

Divisions of continuing higher education (CHE) are organizational subunits of the university. Because they operate at the periphery of the institution, connecting the institution with elements outside it, they are also boundary-spanning subunits (Leifer & Delbecq, 1978; Pedersen & Fleming, 1981; Knox, 1982). In spanning the boundary of the institution, CHE units and their personnel perform three major categories of activities:

1. They process and transmit to others information gathered from the parent organization and from the external, community environment.
2. They identify and secure resources (e.g., funding, participants, political goodwill, philosophical support) needed for the work of the CHE unit and the university.
3. They participate in determining (1) the university's boundary, especially by identifying and working with clients who in turn become participants in the institution, and (2) the university's work domain or what it counts as legitimate work in terms of programs (Jemison, 1984).

As boundary spanners, both the continuing education unit and its personnel play a critical role in anticipating and dealing with environmental change as it affects the university (Pedersen & Fleming, 1981). This boundary-spanning function, and sophistication in performing it, become even more essential as environmental complexity, uncertainty, and hetero-geneity increase (Aldrich, 1979; Scott, 1987). The coming demographic changes and cultural suffusion described earlier point to increased environ-mental complexity, heterogeneity, and uncertainty for the university, and, in turn, to the vital role continuing education can play in dealing with these challenges.

Boundaries of systems, whether physical, biological, or organizational, are recognized as places where there is much richness and complexity. In organizations, this richness comes in the form of environmental change and complexity, and in the heterogeneity of ideas, values, and perspectives increasingly prevalent in organizational environments. Continuing educa-tors' presence at the institution's boundary, where richness and complexity increasingly abound, places them at a strategic location where many critical contributions can be made to the institution and its long-term effectiveness and health. Continuing educators can be collectors, processors, and trans-mitters of information essential to the institution's functioning and to im-portant external constituencies' interpretations and understanding of insti-tutional missions and actions. They can serve as mirrors for institutional self-evaluation, contributing to the institution's understanding of how rele-vant and diverse external stakeholders perceive and value it. And they can join, in meaningful ways, in helping the institution define who, including diverse groups, participates in the life of the institution and what types of programs and services it offers for those groups.

Although the boundary-spanning role is critical, and will become even more so, continuing education units have yet to convince parent organiza-tions of their potential contributions in this particular area (Votruba, 1987). One reason for this state of affairs is that continuing education has failed to appreciate fully its boundary-spanning role and to develop its boundary-spanning capacity for its own fuller benefit and that of the parent organiza-tion. Continuing education could correct this situation by organizing itself so it can (a) be flexible enough to evolve along with changing environmental circumstances so that its responsiveness and leadership are enhanced, and (b) learn how to learn from the increasingly heterogeneous and uncertain environment in which it finds itself.

Organizational Flexibility and Responsiveness

In his treatment of *Images of Organization*, Morgan (1986) uses holo-graphic design as a metaphor to demonstrate one way in which this organi-zational flexibility, change, and learning can be fostered. A hologram is a picture in which the entire image portrayed is contained within each of its parts. Consequently, illuminating any piece of the hologram will produce the entire image. This is possible because information about the whole image is distributed throughout its parts (total distributedness) and because every piece of the image is interconnected. From an organizational perspective, then, holographic design requires (a) that what is central to the organization be contained within each of its parts, (b) that the parts be interconnected and redundant, and (c) that both specialization and generalization be simultaneously present within the organization (Morgan, 1986). According to Morgan, four principles of organization are required in holographic organizational design:

1. Redundancy of functions;
2. Requisite variety;
3. Minimum critical specification; and
4. Learning to learn.

These facilitate self-organization, or the process by which an organization's "structure and function can evolve along with changing circumstances" (p. 96).

The rapidity of change in society and within institutions of higher education will require organizations of continuing higher education to adapt quickly and effectively to the changes in their two task environments — the service area and the parent institution. Each of the four principles described by Morgan provides a means by which the continuing education unit can deal effectively with its boundary-spanning role and address the many issues that increased cultural diversity will raise.

Redundancy of functions.   The first design principle is redundancy of functions. According to this principle, the professional staff of continuing education units should possess multiple skills that enable them to perform another's jobs and substitute for one other as needed. Instead of relying on individuals specialized in needs assessment, program design, or marketing to carry out *only* their specialized tasks (an "assembly-line" work method in which each individual's work contributes independently to the whole), a unit could make individual staff members responsible, for example, for carrying out this range of activities for the academic departments or client groups with which they work. But a given individual would not necessarily be limited to working with selected academic departments or client groups. Others would also possess sufficient knowledge and skills to substitute for the individual if workload demands required it. Even if specialists were needed in the unit, their contributions would be employed and modified within the context of others' contributions, rather than being relied upon in an assembly-line manner of doing work. In this way the core functions of the whole are built into the parts (or into each staff member), thereby meeting the definition of holographic design.

This principle allows for job enrichment (Herzberg, 1968) and the application of principles of Janowitz's (1969) aggregation model. Job enrichment means assigning tasks involving responsibility and autonomy to the employee rather than merely adding new tasks to a person's job (which Herzberg labels job enlargement). Job enrichment also calls for vertical enlargement of a job so that some of the decision-making authority of higher levels is delegated to, or at least shared with, those at lower levels of the organization.

Janowitz's (1969) aggregation model was developed to deal with what he perceived to be overspecialization in urban schools. The model provides for flexible role boundaries among staff and aggregation of functions within roles rather than division of functions according to narrow areas of specialization. Bennis and Slater (1968), in their call for temporary ad hoc groups to deal with changing situations, carry Janowitz's model to its logical conclusion (Katz & Kahn, 1978). By this means, jobs are enriched, functions are aggregated in roles, and temporary assignments of staff are created to deal with the changing requirements of the external environment.

Actions taken to comply with the principle of redundancy of function would result in holographic staffing patterns, since capacities relevant to the core functions of the continuing education operation (the whole) would be built into the role of each staff member (the parts). In addition, the staff's discretionary power and engagement in a variety of functions would be valued over centralized control and overspecialization. Specialization might still be necessary but would be employed in a holographic, instead of assembly-line, fashion in contributing to the core work of the unit. Implementing this principle also facilitates the development of project teams much like those employed in King and Lerner's (1987) integrated model of continuing education organization. Project teams permit overlapping skills and knowledge, as well as including specialized knowledge and skills as necessary, since it is unlikely that everyone can be trained in all continuing education functions (Morgan, 1986). As a result, staff would be able to interface more effectively, through these project teams, with the multiplicity of cultures within and outside the parent institution as environmental conditions and demands warranted.

Requisite variety. The second principle is Asby's (1960) idea of requisite variety, which argues for the "proactive embracing of the environment in all its diversity" (Morgan, 1986, p. 101). According to this principle, as cultures suffuse, the employment of culturally diverse individuals in continuing education will be not only a moral imperative but an organizational one as well. People must be employed who will help the organization to recognize and articulate the problems it faces. On the basis of this principle, heterogeneity and diversity are valued over homogeneity and a single way of viewing the organization's environment.

Heterogeneous staffing patterns will be required so that information collected from continuing education's environments will be as representative as possible, and so that environments can be perceived in their full diversity and complexity. According to Weick (1979), "selecting" is the process by which organizations and their members use attitudes, beliefs, and cognitive templates, stencils, or scripts to make equivocal organizational environments unequivocal or sensible. Organizations and their members simply select certain information to which they will attend, and discard other information. A heterogeneous staff will help to ensure that the attitudes, beliefs, and frameworks used to define the environment will better reflect that environment than would be the case if staffing were homogeneous.

An example will illustrate the potential for applying this principle. Continuing education is an area of higher education in which women have been employed in growing numbers. Kramer (1989) notes that continuing education's contributions to access and programming for women may be one of its noblest accomplishments in this century. Would this contribution have been made if women had not been employed in significant numbers in continuing education units? Research suggests that the entry of increasing numbers of women into the ranks of continuing education has fostered continuing education's contributions to women's educational access and opportunity and to programs developed specifically for this client group. Adam and Lindoo (1989) found, for instance, that female program staff appear to be more sensitive to women's educational needs and concerns than are continuing education deans and directors, whose positions continue to be held primarily by men. A similar influx of minorities into continuing education positions will be required to introduce into the continuing education organization ideas and ways of thinking that are reflective of minority needs. In this way continuing education will be able to be sensitive to the cultural diversity in, and to select information from, its increasingly heterogeneous environment.

The visible presence of women and minorities is also necessary for the development of an environment conducive to recruiting and retaining minority groups in continuing education programs. As we noted earlier, organizations, including organizations of continuing education, will have to compete for employees who are characterized by their diversity. However, the principle of requisite variety focuses on something different than this element of competition for productive workers. It highlights the need to do so to enrich the organization in order for it to understand and be able to respond to the very heterogeneity out of which employees are drawn.

Redundancy of functions and the participation of women and minorities in continuing education are necessary but insufficient conditions for developing the kind of boundary-spanning unit that can assist higher education in dealing with the evolving, uncertain, and increasingly heterogeneous environment of which it is a part. For the unit to realize its capacity for self-organization and for the generation of new understandings and actions, the principles of minimum critical specification and learning to learn must also be implemented.

Minimum critical specification. The principle of minimum critical specification argues for a focus on inquiry-driven behavior rather than on prespecified design. It "attempts to preserve flexibility by suggesting that, in general, one should specify no more than is absolutely necessary for a particular activity to occur" (Morgan, 1986, p. 101). Leaders of continuing education units should foster conditions within their units that encourage and facilitate flexible and varied, rather than rigid and habitual, approaches to problems and needs. Activities such as environmental scanning, strategic planning, and program planning should not be so rigidly orchestrated that the unit cannot respond flexibly and appropriately to changing environmental conditions. However, if it is improperly implemented, this principle can result in chaotic attempts to respond to changing environmental conditions. To control for the possibility of chaos, Morgan (1986) recommends the development of learning systems in which the unit not only learns from its environment but also learns how to learn.

Learning to learn. Continuing educators have traditionally attempted to learn about their environments and to obtain feedback about their programs. Articles and texts are replete with information about how to scan the environment for information, conduct internal audits, and evaluate programs. These functions, however, customarily address the lower-level, or single-loop, form of organizational learning. In this form of learning the primary focus is on using information, judged against existing criteria or norms, to make corrections in system operations Argyris & Schon, 1978; Fiol & Lyles, 1985). Negative feedback is valued most because only through the acquisition of such feedback can corrections be made. Positive feedback is less useful because it merely reinforces what is currently being done (Katz & Kahn, 1978).

Although important to continuing educators, lower-level or single-loop learning is limited because it does not provide individuals or organizations with a basis for inquiring into or challenging the prevailing norms, criteria, and assumptions with which the organizational unit works. As cultures continue to suffuse, continuing education will increasingly need to emphasize higher-level learning, or what Argyris and Schon (1978) call double-loop learning, over single-loop or lower-level learning. In double-loop learning, operating norms and standards of action are open to question so that they can be changed as environmental conditions evolve. Combined with the principles of redundancy of functions, requisite variety, and minimum critical specification, higher-level learning equips continuing education units to become enabling, flexible learning centers for their parent institutions. Inquiry about the norms and operating assumptions by all within the organization, and openness to the expression of heterogeneous views, including those held by minority individuals, can be fostered instead of maintenance of the status quo and reliance on dominant, homogeneous perspectives.

Fostering Cross-Cultural Learning

Emphasizing double-loop learning, especially if it is to be cross-cultural in nature, is, however, no easy task. Several barriers can prevent organizations from learning at a higher level and thereby from tapping the potential of such learning. Some of the barriers that follow from the principles considered above are:

1. *Over-bureaucratization and specialization*, which result from maximum critical specification and lack of redundancy of functions, create situations in which individuals are constrained by role definitions and expectations from making innovative contributions to the organization. Unique individual learning and insights, though possible, frequently do not manifest themselves in action because social norms and accountability criteria encourage maintenance of the status quo and discourage action based on challenges to organizational customs and norms (March & Olsen, 1975; Morgan, 1986).

2. *Gaps between what people say they do and what they actually do* (what Argyris & Schon [1974] identify as the difference between "espoused theory" and "theory in use") are reflected in distinctions between problems that are usually addressed and problems that should be addressed in double-loop learning. Another manifestation of this phenomenon is evident in what Argyris (1986) has labeled "organizational defensive routines," or "any policies or actions that prevent the organization from experiencing pain or threat *and* simultaneously prevent learning how to correct the causes of the threat in the first place" (p. 541). These routines, which inhibit challenges to basic assumptions and norms, are, according to Argyris, "pro overprotection" and "anti learning."

An earlier-mentioned example of defensive routines in continuing education is the field's rationalizations for low involvement of underrepresented groups in programs (Kramer, 1989). Defensive routines also frequently manifest themselves within the organization as mixed messages, which can be especially problematic for minority groups. Research suggests, for example, that race is related to negative job performance evaluations for African-American managers. In addition, these effects of race seem to be related to (a) the lack of decision-making authority accorded these managers and (b) their lower level of acceptance within the organization (Greenhaus, Parasuraman, & Wormley, 1990). These two realities generate mixed messages such as "You were hired because of your competence, but you are not trusted to make important decisions" or "You are valued by management but not by the organization" (Martin & Ross-Gordon, 1990, p. 51). Such messages can blunt the full and ready acceptance of minority group members within the unit, and in turn the valuable contributions they can make to the organization's higher-level learning. Therefore, defensive routines like these and others can interfere gravely with double-loop learning in an organizational unit characterized by cultural diversity.

3. *Ossification of group norms and values* tends to occur over time and can deter higher-level learning. The influx into an organization of diverse individuals with different ways of thinking can do much to introduce new ideas that help a group reconsider its basic norms and assumptions. However, all groups exercise a more or less continuous selection pressure in favor of compliance and sociability (van der Molen, 1989). New individuals may become members of a newly negotiated order, grow alienated from the group and thereby contribute little to its overall belief system and in turn to its learning, or eventually leave the group, having found the cost of compliance too high (March & Olsen, 1975). To develop and maintain a culturally diverse work group, the continuing education administrator must therefore explore ways to avoid ossified ways of thinking, while simultaneously averting the negative consequences of alienation.

4. *A lack of focus on noxiants in the environment* can interfere with double-loop learning. Higher-level learning by definition questions the limits that are placed on action, whether as a result of the beliefs, attitudes, and norms of the work group or because of constraints imposed on the unit by its environment (Morgan, 1986). In contrast to lower-level learning, which is concerned with success or failure in meeting goals and objectives and is thereby constrained by the goals and objectives themselves, higher-level learning dares to question goals and objectives and the values and norms upon which they rest.

In addition, higher-level learning does not consider environmental constraints and demands as givens, but rather seeks first to identify and then to reduce, if not remove, them. To the extent possible, continuing educators should seek to push back constraints and reduce demands, thereby increasing the quantity, improving the quality, and expanding the types of choices available to them (Donaldson, 1990). Higher-level organizational learning draws our attention to the wisdom of defining and challenging constraints and demands, whereby we create the opportunity to choose from among the limits we wish to avoid rather than merely choosing from among the ends we wish to achieve (Morgan, 1986).

The continuing education administrator can, however, foster higher-level, cross-cultural organizational learning in spite of these barriers. The following guidelines are offered for developing and nurturing this higher-order learning approach in continuing education. Leaders of continuing higher education units should:

1. Encourage and value openness and reflectiveness among their staff members and recognize that uncertainty, ambiguity, and errors are inevitable features of organizational life (Morgan, 1986).
2. Vary, to the extent that staff size permits, the membership of working groups created to deal with issues and problems. This guideline, which involves implementing the principle of redundancy of functions, will do much to prevent the ossification of ideas within social groups. However, as we mentioned earlier in relation to the work force in general, this too will mean that continuing educators will have to be prepared to work in groups that place greater demands on cross-cultural communication and interpersonal skills (Goddard, 1989).
3. Combine a focus on inquiry-driven behavior with a focus on the professional and personal development of staff, especially women and minority group staff members, so that their contributions to the life and learning of the organization can be encouraged, supported, and nurtured. More particularly, professional development opportunities should be offered that emphasize and capitalize on the strengths and different perspectives that women and minorities bring with them into continuing education. Professional development will also have to focus on cross-cultural communication and interpersonal skills so that work in the flexible and frequently reconstructed work groups recommended above can be made as effective as possible. Without such a focus the potential for new ideas and new ways of thinking will be diminished.
4. Encourage an approach to the analysis and solution of complex problems that recognizes the importance of exploring different viewpoints (Morgan, 1986).
5. Promote participative, bottom-up planning and problem identification. This will permit goals and objectives to arise from norms and values identified through ongoing dialogue, rather than letting norms and values be defined by existing goals and objectives (Senge, 1990).

6. Focus not only on ends but also on limits to action so that choices can be made about the limits the organization wants to avoid as well as the ends it wants to achieve.

Higher-order organizational learning will enable the continuing education unit to reflect society's cultural diversity more fully and help the parent institution to respond appropriately to that diversity. Achieving this level of learning will, however, require reorganizing the work of continuing education. The principles and ideas that have been outlined provide ways for continuing education to enhance its boundary-spanning role, for its organization and function to evolve more effectively with a changing environment, and for its capacity for higher-order organizational learning to be strengthened. Taken together, the principles and ideas also suggest a way in which this higher-order learning can be cross-cultural. This type of learning will be required if continuing education units are to view their environments in their richness and complexity and become increasingly responsive to cultural diversity.

CONCLUSION

Continuing education, like many segments of higher education and society, has developed its own mythology to explain its lack of involvement in and responsiveness to the cultural diversity that increasingly surrounds it. A review of demographic trends and enrollment patterns has indicated, however, that we can no longer rely on the argument that continuing higher education's mission of the "higher learnings" prevents it from serving more egalitarian purposes. Learners of diverse backgrounds do have the backgrounds and motivation required for continuing higher education, even if the most stringent norms of higher education remain unchanged. The mythology also precludes the development of creative and innovative programs that enable continuing education to reach underserved groups within the context of higher education's major aims and standards. The programs described earlier in this chapter are in the vanguard of innovative approaches to addressing this situation, taking us beyond our rationalizations and defensive routines.

But understanding the demographics and developing a few innovative programs will not be enough. There is a critical need for alternatives to traditional ways of organizing and doing continuing education's work, especially as both ethnic and professional cultures continue to suffuse. The holographic organizational design is an alternative means for continuing education units to deal with this rapidly changing environment and to become more effective boundary-spanning units within the university. Continuing education's boundary-spanning function is essential. Where this function can be enhanced, continuing education will be in a position both to better serve and to gain influence within its parent organization and its various external, culturally diverse constituencies.

King and Lerner (1987) propose an integrated organizational model for continuing education that "combines an interest in entrepreneurial success with a concern for academic rigor and innovativeness" (p. 32). The model is bicultural with respect to internal and external environments. Like the Roman god Janus, members of the integrated model of continuing education organizations simultaneously face inward and outward, having accepted core values of both environments and acting to facilitate a dialectical process by which actions are determined within the context of conflicting, diverse values. As King and Lerner note, the continuing education unit becomes the intellectual "front parlor" of the university, a place where people come together to share and discuss often divergent ideas.

To the extent to which continuing education organizations become more diverse, and, acting on the principles of holographic design, create an organizational capacity for learning (Morgan, 1986), continuing higher education can aspire to become the "front parlor" of the university. Reaching this goal depends on continuing education's ability to become an enhancing, cross-cultural subculture of the organization and society at large, a subculture that values differences and their exploration within the context of environmental uncertainty, heterogeneity, and cultural suffusion. Building a shared sense of this new cross-culture into each and every continuing educator will serve yet another holographic function: the creation of the coherence and integrity required for a continuing education unit to make major contributions to higher education and to society and its diverse populations.

REFERENCES

Adam, K., & Lindoo, S. (1989). Continuing education programs for women: Current status and future directions. *Continuing Higher Education Review, 53*(1), 11–25.

Aldrich, H. E. (1979). *Organizations and environments*. Englewood Cliffs, NJ: Prentice-Hall.

American Association of State Colleges and Universities & National Association of State Universities and Land Grant Colleges. (1986). *Public four-year colleges and universities: A healthy enrollment environment*. Washington, DC: Author.

Argyris, C. (1986). Reinforcing organizational defensive routines: An unintended human resources activity. *Human Resource Management, 25*(4), 541–555.

Argyris, C., & Schon, D. A. (1974). *Theory in Practice*. San Francisco: Jossey-Bass.

Argyris, C., & Schon, D. A. (1978). *Organizational learning: A theory of action perspective.* Reading, MA: Addison-Wesley.

Asby, W. R. (1960). *An introduction to cybernetics.* London: Chapman & Hall.

Aslanian, C. B. (1990). *Back from the future.* Unpublished manuscript. Presented at the National University Continuing Education Association, New Orleans, LA.

Baker, C. O., & Thompson, G. R. (Eds.) (1989). *The condition of education, 1989* (Vol. 1). National Center for Education Statistics. Washington, DC: U.S. Government Printing Office.

Beaty, J., & Chiste, K. B. (1986). University preparation for Native American students: Theory and application. *Journal of American Indian Education, 40*(3), 6–13.

Bennis, W. G., & Slater, P. E. (1968). *The temporary society.* New York: Harper & Row.

Briscoe, D. B., & Ross, J. M. (1989). Racial and ethnic minorities and adult education. In S. B. Merriam & P. M. Cunningham (Eds.), *Handbook of adult and continuing education* (pp. 583–598). San Francisco: Jossey-Bass.

Bruno, R. (1990). *School enrollment—Social and economic characteristics of students: October 1988 and 1987.* Current Population Reports, Population Characteristics series, No. 443, p. 20. Washington, DC: U.S. Bureau of the Census.

Cain, R. A. (1987). Counseling African-American adult learners. *The Journal of Continuing Higher Education, 35*(2), 25–28.

Carnevale, A. P. (1989). The learning enterprise. *Training and Development Journal, 43*(2), 26–33.

Carroll, D. (1989). *College persisters and degree attainment for 1980 high school graduates: Hazards for transfers, stop-outs, and part-timers.* National Center for Education Statistics. Washington, DC: U.S. Government Printing Office.

Continuing Education develops responses to America's new cultural diversity. (1990–1991, Dec.–Jan.) *NUCEA News, 7*(1), 1, 6.

Copeland, L. (1988). Learning to manage a multicultural work force. *Training, 25*(5), 49–56.

Donaldson, J. F. (1990). *Managing credit programs in continuing higher education.* Urbana, IL: University of Illinois.

Fiol, C. M., & Lyles, M. A. (1985). Organizational learning. *Academy of Management Review, 10*(4), 803–813.

Goddard, R. W. (1989). Work force 2000. *Personnel Journal, 68*(2), 65–71.

Greenhaus, J. F., Parasuraman, S., & Wormly, W. M. (1990). Effects of race on organizational experiences, job performance evaluations, and career outcomes. *Academy of Management Journal, 33*(1), 64–86.

Henry, M. D. (1985). Black reentry females: Their concerns and needs. *Journal of the National Association of Women Deans, Administrators and Counselors, 48*(4), 5–10.

Herzberg, F. (1968). One more time: How do you motivate employees? *Harvard Business Review, 46,* 53–62.

Hill, S. T. (1987). *Trends in Adult Education, 1969–1984,* Office of Educational

Improvement, Center for Education Statistics. Washington, DC: U.S. Government Printing Office (ERIC Document Reproduction Service No. ED 282 054).

Hodgkinson, H. L. (1985). Demographics and the economy: Understanding a changing marketplace. *The Admissions strategist. Recruiting for the 1980s, no. 3.* Special issue on adult recruitment. New York: The College Board.

Janowitz, M. (1969). *Institution building in urban education.* New York: Russell Sage Foundation.

Jemison, D. B. (1984). The importance of boundary spanning roles in strategic decision making. *Journal of Management Studies, 21*(2), 131–152.

Katz, D., & Kahn, R. L. (1978). *The social psychology of organizations* (2nd ed.). New York: Wiley.

King, B. K., & Lerner, A. W. (1987). Organization structure and performance dynamics in continuing education administration. *Continuing Higher Education Review, 51*(3), 21–38.

Knox, A. B. (1981). The continuing education agency and its parent organization. In J. C. Votruba (Ed.), *Strengthening internal support for continuing education, New directions for continuing education, no. 9* (pp. 1–11). San Francisco: Jossey-Bass.

Knox, A. B. (1982). *Leadership strategies for meeting new challenges, New directions for continuing education, no. 13.* San Francisco: Jossey-Bass.

Kominski, R. (1988). *Educational attainment in the United States: March 1987 and 1986.* Current population reports. Washington, DC: U.S. Dept. of Commerce, Bureau of the Census.

Kramer, J. L. (1989). Continuing education in a multicultural society: Challenges of access and environment. *The Journal of Continuing Higher Education, 37*(1), 2–4.

Leifer, R. P., & Delbecq, A. (1978). Organizational/environmental interchange: A model of boundary spanning activity. *Academy of Management Review, 3,* 40–50.

Magner, D. K. (1990, January 17). Enrollment of blacks and Hispanics found to rise fitfully over 2 years. *Chronicle of Higher Education, 36*(18), p. 3.

March, J. G., & Olsen, J. P. (1975). The uncertainty of the past: Organizational learning under ambiguity. *European Journal of Political Research, 3,* 147–171.

Martin, L. G., & Ross-Gordon, J. M. (1990). Cultural diversity in the workplace: Managing a multicultural work force. In J. M. Ross-Gordon, L. G. Martin, & D. B. Briscoe (Eds.), *Serving culturally diverse populations, New directions for adult and continuing education, no. 48* (pp. 45–54). San Francisco: Jossey-Bass.

Moe, J. F. (1989). The dream deferred: Minority adult participation in higher education in the United States. *Continuing Higher Education Review, 53*(1), 35–49.

Morgan, G. (1982). Cybernetics and organization theory: Epistemology or technique? *Human Relations, 35*(7), 521–537.

Morgan, G. (1986). *Images of organization.* Beverly Hills, CA: Sage.

National Alliance of Business. (1986). *Employment Policies: Looking to the year 2000*. Washington, DC: National Alliance of Business.

National Center for Educational Statistics. (1986). *Projected decline in college enrollment not materializing*. Washington, DC: U.S. Department of Education.

National Center for Educational Statistics. (1988). *National estimates of higher education: School year 1988-89*. Washington, DC: U.S. Department of Education.

Nussbaum, B. (1988, September 19). Needed: Human capital. *Business Week*, pp. 100-103.

O'Brien, E. M. (1990, March 1). Continuing ed programs not reaching minority populations, officials admit. *Black issues in Higher Education*, 6-8.

Part-time students account for the majority of all graduate level enrollments. (1990, April). *NUCEA News, 4*(4), 3.

Part-time higher education enrollments climb throughout the eighties. (1990, February). *NUCEA News, 6*(2), 3.

Part-time enrollments projected to increase gradually in the 1990s. (1990, April). *NUCEA News, 6*(4), 3.

Part-time students account for the majority of all graduate level enrollments. (1988, April 1). *NUCEA News, 4*(4), 3.

Pedersen, K. G., & Fleming, T. (1981). The academic organization and continuing education. *Canadian Journal of University Continuing Education, 7*(2), 4-9.

Scott, W. R. (1987). *Organizations: Rational, natural, and open systems* (2nd ed.). Englewood Cliffs, NJ: Prentice-Hall.

Senge, P. M. (1990). *The fifth discipline: The art and practice of the learning organization*. New York: Doubleday.

Snyder, T. (1988). *Digest of education statistics*. Office of Educational Research and Improvement and the National Center for Education Statistics. Washington, DC: Government Printing Office.

Solomon, C. M. (1989). The corporate responses to work force diversity. *Personnel Journal, 68*(8), 43-53.

Surrey, D., & Perry, R. (1986). Urban, poor, female and returning to school: Providing for the *advantaged* urban adult. In *Proceedings of the National Conference on the Adult Learner*. Columbia: University of South Carolina.

The Asian population boom. (1990, March 14). *Education Week*, p. 3.

U.S. Bureau of the Census. (1989). *Statistical abstracts of the United States, 1989*. Washington, DC: Department of Commerce.

van der Molen, P. P. (1989). Adaptation-innovation and changes in social structure: On the anatomy of catastrophe. In M. J. Kirton (Ed.), *Adaptors and innovators: Styles of creativity and problem solving* (pp. 158-199). New York: Routledge.

Votruba, J. C. (1987). From marginality to mainstream: Strategies for increasing internal support for continuing education. In R. G. Simerly & Associates, *Strategic planning and leadership in continuing education* (pp. 185-201). San Francisco: Jossey-Bass.

Weick, K. E. (1979). *The social psychology of organizing*. Reading, MA: Addison-Wesley.

Wilson, R., & Carter, D. J. (1988). *Seventh annual status report on minorities in higher education*. Washington, DC: American Council on Education.

Zemsky, R. (1983). Summary findings. In R. Zemsky, M. Tierney, I. Berg, & J. Shack-Marquez (1983), *Training's benchmarks. A statistical sketch of employer-provided training and education 1969–1981. Task I Report: The impact of public policy on education and training in the private sector*. Philadelphia: Pennsylvania University, Higher Education Finance Research Institute (ERIC Document Reproduction No. ED 265 379).

3

Change in Continuing Higher Education: Implications for Faculty

Marcia D. Escott
William D. Semlak
Mark E. Comadena

Our society is being rapidly transformed by trends such as advancing technology, the uncertainty over national priorities, and the restructuring of the American economy. The United States is shifting from a manufacturing economy to a high-technology manufacturing, information, and service economy. The political, economic, social, international, and technological environment is changing, and these changes are affecting continuing higher education.

Throughout this chapter, we will refer to a "wave of change" in continuing education. This metaphor symbolizes the inevitable, sweeping changes that are occurring in our society and affecting higher continuing education. This wave of change, which sometimes seems a mere ripple and at other times a powerful breaker, is buffeting academe. In short, society is placing greater demands on higher education to offer solutions to the problems of our world.

This chapter will address the impact that changes in continuing higher education will have on faculty. The chapter begins with a discussion of the evolving university mission, by presenting a historical overview of the traditional tripartite mission of higher education—teaching, research, and service—and its effect on the role of faculty. We will demonstrate that the mission of higher continuing education creates a pressure on the hierarchy of value placed on each of these three components. Next, we will review the traditional role of faculty, showing that faculty in general view themselves as working in an insulated environment and see their role in a very traditional sense. The chapter will then introduce the notion that continuing higher education units serve most colleges and universities as a window through which the institution is exposed to environmental change. While continuing education is not the only such window for a university, it is clearly an important one, through which many faculty experience the outside world's demands on academe. The chapter concludes with a research-based discussion of the new student and how that student differs from the traditional student. We argue that faculty must change their pedagogical procedures if these are to be effective with the students who are entering today's continuing higher education programs.

THE EVOLVING UNIVERSITY MISSION

Most four-year institutions of higher learning profess a tripartite mission of teaching, research, and service. The role of faculty is generally defined by the same triad. Depending on an institution's focus, one of these three functions may be emphasized over another. Yet, despite differing organizational objectives, institutions of higher education tend to treat the triad as a hierarchy of values. At most large state universities and major private institutions research is the primary gauge by which individual faculty merit is measured and by which the institution judges its effectiveness. A "publish or perish" philosophy drives these institutions and has become an accepted way of life for faculty who expect to be tenured and promoted at such schools. Yet, despite overwhelming adherence to this concept, not all agree that it is best for higher education. Donald Kennedy, president of Stanford University, recently stated, "It is time for us to reaffirm that education—that is, teaching in all its forms—is the primary task of higher education" (cited in Boyer, 1990, p. 1).

If we look at higher education from a historical perspective, research does not always dominate a faculty member's tripartite role. The history of higher education in America shows that teaching and service have both been important elements of higher education. Even today, for some segments of major universities, notably continuing education units, teaching and service are prized components of the educational mission.

From the days of Chaucer's *Canterbury Tales*, when a teacher gladly taught and a pupil gladly learned, to the present, the emphasis placed on teaching, research, and service, respectively, has varied with the times. In his recent report titled *Scholarship Reconsidered: Priorities of the Professoriate* (1990), Ernest L. Boyer describes how both teaching and service have been highly valued at various times in our history. In colonial times, the faculty's mission was to build men of character who would assume religious and civic leadership positions. Teaching was assumed to be a profession that emerged from a sacred calling and was treated on a par with that of the ministry. David Tyack, in describing the founding of Harvard College in 1636, stated that the faculty had the noble task of advancing learning and transmitting it to posterity (cited in Boyer, 1990, p. 3). The privileged could send their children to early American institutions and be confident of finding a dedicated faculty who would serve as both teachers and role models.

As education developed in America, the faculty, in addition to its teaching role, assumed other roles more closely associated with a service function. As the country expanded, various practical needs emerged and were addressed by universities. Practical solutions were needed for the problems associated with building a new nation, such as constructing bridges, expanding railroads, and developing manufacturing. In 1824, Rensselaer Polytechnic Institute, one of our nation's first technical schools, was founded and became a mecca for technological problem-solving. Some 20 years later, Yale University developed course offerings in agricultural chemistry to study issues related to the growing need to feed the public and to develop agriculture as an economic enterprise. During this period, even Harvard University began to stress that part of its mission was to serve business and help provide solutions to the growing problems of commerce (Boyer, 1990).

The Morrill Acts of 1862 and 1890 also spurred institutions to develop their public service function. Considerable emphasis was placed on developing "cow colleges" that stressed training in agriculture and mechanical skills. The Morrill Acts provided public funds to colleges and universities for developing curricula and service programs designed to meet the needs of a growing economy. During this period the relationship between education and economic development helped foster a perception that public colleges and universities benefited society and, in fact, represented desirable investments in the future. Land grant institutions received broad public support because the economic benefits from these institutions exceeded the dollars invested in them (Strand, 1990).

Thomas Larson (1989) described the land grant movement as responsible for creating "new uses for the university." From their inception, land grant institutions were designed to play a pivotal role in the economic development of the states and nation. The faculty at these institutions took a lead in researching issues related to agricultural improvements, while the agricultural extension agents supported and trained by these land grant schools served as change agents working with farmers to apply the latest scientific farming methods. The United States' prominence in agriculture can be traced to the research and extension efforts of land grant universities and the U.S. Department of Agriculture's support and encouragement of those efforts.

Thus, by the late 1800s, a perception of the mission of the university included the belief that universities should help to train future leaders and support the growing economy. This expectation would be expanded in a new and important way.

Almost 100 years earlier, Thomas Jefferson had articulated the belief that the purpose of education was to create an educated and informed public. While this idea was accepted at the conceptual level, not until the end of the nineteenth century, with the coming of the lyceum movement, was it actually implemented. The lyceum movement focused attention on the need to disseminate practical information and raise the general level of social morality. This was to be achieved by providing a general education for the public at large, rather than just for the elite. The lyceum movement thus went a step further than the common school movement, which called on colleges and universities to place greater emphasis on general and practical education that would produce not only a moral public but a practically skilled citizenry as well. Consistent with these ideas was a view of the faculty performing a dual role—teaching and service.

Thus a clearly defined view of the teaching and service role of the faculty emerged. The importance of teaching was voiced by Charles Eliot when he assumed the presidency of Harvard University in 1869 and declared that "The prime business of American professors . . . must be regular and assiduous class teaching" (cited in Boyer, 1990, p. 4). By 1908, Eliot further claimed that "At bottom most of the American institutions of higher education are filled with the modern democratic spirit of serviceableness. Teachers and students alike are profoundly moved by the desire to serve the democratic community" (cited in Boyer, 1990, p. 5).

While the teaching and service roles of universities were evolving on this side of the Atlantic, a different view of the university was developing in Europe. At the German university, considerable emphasis was placed on research. In fact, G. Stanley Hall, president of Clark University, wrote in 1891, "The German university is today the freest spot on earth . . . nowhere has the passion to push on to the frontier of human knowledge been so general" (cited in Boyer, 1990, p. 8). German universities developed the notion that a professor needs to view the everyday world from a distance.

A new emphasis on basic research was also spreading to the United States. Of colonial times, Dael Wolfle wrote: "Professors were hired to teach the science that was already known—to add to that knowledge was not expected. . . . " (cited in Boyer, 1990, p. 8). In 1861, the Massachusetts Institute of Technology (MIT) was founded as a center for the study of scientific activity. Other institutions followed and by the late 1800s, the

University of Chicago used research productivity as a major criterion in the promotion of faculty (Boyer, 1990).

Thus by the twentieth century teaching, research, and service had emerged in the United States as critical components of the mission of higher education. During the following decades changes in the external world and the expectations placed on institutions of higher education continued to influence the mission of these institutions and the role of faculty. After World War II, President Truman appointed a Commission on Higher Education that recommended that the mission of higher education be modified. Once again, higher education was called on to serve not just the elite, but the masses. The GI Bill opened the financial doors of higher education to a broad spectrum of middle- and lower-class citizens who viewed the educational opportunities provided by higher education as a right, not a privilege.

Since World War II, the role of the large public and land grant universities has continued to evolve. During the early postwar period these universities were asked to provide leadership in conducting basic research. Federal and corporate monies were channeled into a variety of highly successful basic research programs. NASA, by building on the results of many of these programs, was able to assemble a substantial space program that led to the spectacular moon landing in 1969.

By the 1960s, the United States had become a leader in the world economy. Corporate engineers were able to apply the results of basic research programs to successful product development. However, other economies, based on other governmental, industrial, and educational models, have since emerged on the world scene. Germany and Japan, for example, are now major players in the world economy.

How have recent changes in the world affected the mission of institutions of higher education and the role of faculty? In colonial times, higher education's primary mission was to teach and to provide moral training for our young elite. In the nineteenth century, service emerged as a primary focus and contributed to our country's technological and economic development. Faculty faced a changing student population created by the Lyceum movement. In the twentieth century, we have seen further technological advances and a surge of adults returning to the classroom to update their job skills, develop leisure activities, and pursue lifelong learning.

Still more change is in the wind. Larson (1989) has called for a major shift in the role of the large land grant public university. Rather than being just a center of basic research, it must become a focal point of applied economic development. Boyer (1990) has stressed that our definition of scholarship must change. He speaks of a scholarship that integrates discovery, application, and teaching. He believes faculty must investigate and discover in order to "advance human knowledge," to make "connections across the disciplines," to apply their findings to solving social problems, and to advance "pedagogical procedures" that will enhance teaching in our colleges and universities. President George Bush has unveiled his plan for a "populist crusade" to reform American schools in which colleges will help to develop elementary and secondary schools and train adults. The proposal calls for educators, business leaders, and scholars to work together in developing "innovative" schools for the future (DeLoughry, 1991). Leaders in business and industry are looking to institutions of higher education for help in retraining their work force. More and more adults are returning to school. Troubled schools, pollution, urban decay, acid rain, AIDS, and the need to retrain our work force are new pressures affecting our universities. How will faculty respond to these external pressures?

THE TRADITIONAL VIEW OF FACULTY

Any attempted definition of the traditional view of faculty is a generalization at best; for every stereotype there is a corresponding exception. Even so, the following observations may be useful for the purposes of this discussion. Most faculty today are white middle-class males who entered the field because of an interest in their subject matter. Most faculty earned their degrees in direct succession and tend to have little experience in other professions. Most, after completing their graduate programs, started teaching in a tenure-track position. They identify teaching areas in which to develop their expertise and research areas in which to produce papers and articles. The more ambitious may receive external grants or publish books. Faculty members generally join professional organizations in their areas of study and attend professional meetings. Most participate in committee work and other service activities at their university.

Faculty members tend to be rather insulated in their contacts and somewhat specialized in their teaching and research. Success often is predicated on teaching in a few narrow areas or researching a very specific aspect of the field. Students consist of 18- to 21-year-olds who come from the same white middle- to upper-class background and espouse the values of that segment of society. Little attention has been devoted to the business and professional community, or to social issues beyond the scope of a faculty member's particular expertise.

Many faculty in this mold found issues such as the civil rights movement or the Vietnam War difficult to deal with. Since their traditional expertise did not cover the issues, they often felt uncomfortable when the issues were raised in an academic setting. While they might have had a personal opinion on the issue, they felt the issue was not germane to the academic setting. These faculty were likewise uncomfortable with vocationalism and career preparation in the academic environment. These changes reflected a disruption of traditional academic values and fostered unreasonable student expectations.

Besides feeling uncomfortable when confronted with issues not related to their area of expertise, many faculty experience what is popularly called burnout. Burnout results from spending too many years teaching the same limited number of courses to the rather homogenous audience described above while researching the same narrow topics and reporting the results at a select number of conferences. Colleges and universities have attempted to fight burnout through sabbaticals and faculty development programs. These programs have had some success but are often limited by financial constraints. In the 1990s, sabbaticals and faculty development programs are likely to be curtailed because of scarce economic resources. In addition, neither is ongoing. At many institutions a sabbatical is granted only every seven years. Faculty development grants are often rotated among faculty and departments so that any individual is unlikely to receive more than one every several years. Both types of programs often bypass the individuals who need them the most because they are awarded on a competitive basis and the most burned-out faculty do not even apply.

These problems are accompanied by a general concern regarding the mission of higher education. Students often complain that what is taught in their academic programs is not relevant to the real world. Employers question the ability of college graduates to succeed in the work force. Governing boards of higher education and legislators question higher education's ability to address the needs of minority populations.

Faculty autonomy is perhaps the crux of this issue. Faculty members largely control what is taught and how it is taught. The curricular process is strongly influenced by faculty interests. Faculty select their research interests and choose what to publish and where and when to publish it. In general, faculty are free to determine what professional organizations they wish to join and how involved in professional organizations they wish to be. Faculty decide whom they will consult in their research and what work outside of the university they will undertake.

At many institutions, the attempt to resolve the problem of faculty autonomy has prompted administrations and governing boards to develop goals for assessment, community outreach, and affirmative action. The result has been that many programs have been diluted or thwarted by faculty who either do not know how to achieve these administration's goals or do not want to change what they teach or how they teach it. Given institutional commitments to academic freedom, the university curricular process, and the reward system associated with a hierarchy of value that exists in tripartite definition of faculty role, change usually does not occur until the faculty initiate the change.

Today many faculty members loosely fit the above stereotype. However, colleges and universities are being exposed to environmental pressures that are making the stereotype increasingly inaccurate. Change is entering colleges and universities through the window of continuing education.

CONTINUING HIGHER EDUCATION: A WINDOW ON THE FUTURE

As we approach the twenty-first century, continuing educators have a unique opportunity to help their institutions and their faculty colleagues meet the demands of the new wave. Continuing educators already have a range of activities underway. These include activities in

> economic development, elementary and secondary education outreach, special services for communities, professional development programs through conferences, institutes and short courses, library lending services, film and visual aid services, summer school programs, extension classes, adult learning/reentry programs, correspondence courses, lecture and cultural series, older adult programs, evening/weekend classes, residence center activities, and broadcasting services. (Strand, 1990, p. 97)

Through these activities and a myriad of others, continuing educators provide opportunities for interdisciplinary approaches to problem-solving. Continuing education programs bring together faculty from various disciplines to address social problems; they link the university with the external community. Continuing educators match the resources of the institution to the needs of the community. In the name of public service, continuing education programs are responding to the demands of the "real" world.

Continuing education programs have the flexibility to allow faculty to be innovative, creative, and entrepreneurial. In these programs, faculty can develop nontraditional courses to be delivered in nontraditional ways to nontraditional student populations. The programs also provide faculty with research opportunities. Continuing educators have been teaching adults for years, often through nontraditional delivery systems and in nontraditional settings; therefore, it is reasonable that they can provide leadership in acquainting their faculty colleagues with the needs of the coming wave of adult learners and the most effective strategies for teaching these learners.

How institutions of higher education will respond to the coming wave and whether faculty will accept the new pressures created by it will depend largely on an institution's organizational structure and the position of continuing education within that structure. The institution's mission must reflect its social and moral responsibility to serve the larger community.

Not all institutions will respond the same way. Some institutions will resist change and will close the window of continuing education because the impact of change on the mission of the institution and on the role of faculty would be very dramatic. Other institutions will permit change, and part of the faculty will respond. These institutions will experience heated debate on their campuses. Faculty who maintain a conventional view will argue for a return to the past and will suggest that the traditional values of the institution be reasserted. Those who espouse the new wave will argue for a redefinition of the institution's mission and for a reward system that supports it. Still other institutions will meet the challenge of the coming wave by opening the window of continuing education; such receptivity will profoundly affect the role of faculty in these institutions.

Just as institutions of higher education will respond to the coming new wave in diverse ways, so will individual faculty members. On one hand, faculty may respond favorably to the myriad possibilities for creating new courses, programs, and teaching strategies. They may welcome the incentives, sometimes financial, for being creative and innovative. They may be pleased with opportunities to collaborate with colleagues from other disciplines, using interdisciplinary approaches to solve real problems. They may be delighted to work with the business and corporate world to meet training needs; they may even value the opportunity to apply research to real social problems, such as AIDS or acid rain.

On the other hand, traditional faculty members may experience change as added pressure. That pressure may affect faculty in a number of ways. While faculty members may be excited about the opportunities afforded through continuing education, the faculty reward system at the institution may still adhere to the traditional hierarchy of values, in which research ranks at the pinnacle of the system, and public service, often ill-defined, is considered to be of little worth. Another source of pressure may be the new student.

THE NEW STUDENT

The traditional faculty member is accustomed to teaching a fairly homogeneous student body. Not only have the demographics of this student body reflected a narrow socioeconomic class, but the students' social and political values have reflected a rather narrow viewpoint. For the traditional faculty member, this has meant presenting the same series of well-rehearsed lectures from the same set of well-worn notes to an undifferentiated body of passive 18- to 21-year-olds, semester after semester.

However, the new wave presents the faculty member with a new student. Typically, this new student is an adult with adult responsibilities, who plays many roles—parent, employee, spouse, to name but a few—in addition to that of student, and whose attendance is generally part-time, even if degree-seeking. The new student represents a population that desires a college or university education but cannot attend classes on the same basis as does the 18- to 21-year-old. Many of these new students face barriers to obtaining higher education.

Institutional barriers may include unavailability of evening classes, strict admission requirements, support systems designed for 18-year-olds, insufficient parking facilities, or a campus that closes at 4:30 p.m. The new student may also face financial barriers; few have the financial means to pursue a college education, and few qualify for the federally funded financial aid packages designed for the traditional college student. Finally, the new student faces personal barriers, such as fear and anxiety about re-entering school or a lack of family support. The new student is often a single parent with outdated job skills, trapped by demands that limit upward mobility and choice. At the same time, that student often represents a segment of the population that up to now has not been considered "college material," either because of mental or physical ability or because of socio-economic or ethnic background. Responding to the new student, a number of institutions have turned to continuing education units to establish programs to ease the entry of such students into higher education.

Faculty members who encounter these nontraditional students in continuing education programs are often confronted with attitudes and behaviors different from those of the traditional student. The initial reaction of many faculty to the changing student body was rejection. In their early stages, many programs graduated students who lacked the intellectual sophistication of some traditional students. Teaching in evening school was left to the lowest-ranking faculty. But faculty attitudes are gradually changing. For example, a study at a major eastern private university indicated that senior tenured faculty considered their adult evening students to be academically on a par with their traditional day students (Shinagel, 1983). In fact, Shinagel reported that over a quarter of the senior faculty teaching in the adult program found teaching in the extension program "more rewarding" than teaching traditional students. Escott, Semlak, and Comadena's (1989) replication of the Shinagel study at a large midwestern state university found similar results. Faculty reported that nontraditional adult students were on a par with traditional students in academic ability. But the faculty noted that the adults were much more motivated and, as a result, performed better in the classroom. The study also found that the faculty members enjoyed teaching adult students and found the experience both challenging and rewarding.

In the classroom, nontraditional students are active, not passive; they participate in class discussion and ask many questions. Research has demonstrated that these students may have less communication apprehension, a higher level of self-esteem, and a more internal locus of control than nontraditional students (Escott, Semlak, & Comadena, 1990). Learning techniques that seemed adequate for teaching the more passive traditional student do not satisfy these populations. Many faculty members who have taught 18- to 21-year-olds for years with great success feel frustrated and confused in a continuing education setting.

Other faculty members, bored by the traditional student's passive attitude toward education, are excited by the nontraditional student. Innovative teaching styles that were of little value in teaching traditional students are "turning on" these nontraditional learners. Approaches such as contract learning, self-paced, competency-based instruction, residential classrooms, and accelerated instruction are being used to teach nontraditional learners. Even faculty members who had settled into a routine while teaching traditional students may be motivated to try new techniques.

Faculty need to adapt their courses and, in particular, their teaching styles to meet the unique needs of the new students. Adult learners are not only older and more experienced, but they appear to possess different social and psychological characteristics. Instructors must be sensitive to these differences and be able to adapt to them. One very clear message emerging from the developing body of research on adult learners shows that adults want to participate actively in the learning process, and that the relationship between instructor and student is very important to them.

How an instructor communicates in the classroom can significantly affect student learning. The essence of instruction is communication. Students and teachers must interact frequently for effective learning to take place (Bloom, 1976; Lysakowski & Walberg, 1982). Factors that interfere with either the quantity or the quality of classroom interaction may hinder both cognitive and affective learning.

A number of factors may affect classroom communication. Students' levels of self-esteem, communication anxiety, and communication competence, for example, may affect their ability and willingness to engage in classroom communication. Students high in self-esteem tend to be low in communication anxiety. These students are more likely to participate in classroom interactions than are students with high communication anxiety. Consequently, they also experience higher levels of cognitive learning

(Comadena & Prusank, 1988). One study (Comadena, Semlak, Looney, & Escott, 1988) found that adult learners possessed significantly higher levels of self-esteem than did traditional undergraduate students.

Another important factor in the classroom communication equation is the teacher's communication style. Communication style refers to "the way one verbally, nonverbally, and paraverbally interacts to signal how literal meaning should be taken, interpreted, filtered, or understood" (Norton, 1978, p. 99). Over the last fifteen years, several studies have examined the relationship between teacher communication style and student evaluations of teacher effectiveness (see Norton, 1977; Andersen, Norton, & Nussbaum, 1979; Norton & Nussbaum, 1980; Nussbaum, Comadena, & Holladay, 1987; Scott & Nussbaum, 1981). These studies, which have been conducted exclusively on traditional undergraduate students, indicate that teachers who are perceived as friendly, relaxed, dramatic, attentive, and open communicators are also perceived as effective teachers and generate high affective evaluations (i.e., liking) from students.

Recently, Escott, Semlak, and Comadena (1990) examined the relationship between communication style and teacher effectiveness in samples of adult learners and traditional undergraduate students. The developing body of literature on the adult learner suggests that adults may prefer different communication styles than do traditional undergraduate students. Knowles (1978), for example, contends that adult learners take an active role in the learning process, participate actively in class activities, actively seek to apply knowledge acquired in class, and prefer a learning climate that shows a concern for student-teacher communication. Knowles states that

> the psychological climate should be one which causes adults to feel accepted, respected, and supported; in which there exists a spirit of mutuality between teachers and students as joint inquirers; in which there is freedom of expression without fear of punishment or ridicule. People tend to feel more "adult" in an atmosphere that is friendly, informal, in which they are known by name and valued as unique individuals, than in the traditional school atmosphere of formality, semianonymity, and status differentiation between teacher and student. (p. 47)

In the Escott, Semlak, and Comadena (1990) study, 182 traditional undergraduate students and 167 adult learners were asked to evaluate an instructor's communication style and to assess the overall effectiveness of that instructor. Teacher effectiveness was operationally defined as an affective evaluation of the instructor. Teacher communication style was measured by having students complete an inventory composed of 45 Likert-type items designed to measure how one verbally and nonverbally interacts with others (Norton, 1983). This inventory measured the extent to which the teacher possessed the following communication styles: friendly, impression-leaving, relaxed, contentious, attentive, precise, animated, dramatic, open, dominant, and communicator image. Results of regression analyses in which communicator style variables served as predictors and teacher effectiveness as the criterion variable revealed that different communication style variables predicted teacher effectiveness in the two groups of students. In the sample of traditional undergraduate students, an effective teacher was one who left a lasting impression on students, and who was friendly and attentive. For adult learners, an effective teacher was on who left a lasting impression on students, and whose communication style was friendly, relaxed, attentive, nondominant, and precise.

Perhaps the most intriguing finding of this study, however, was the relative importance of teacher communication style in predicting teacher effectiveness in the two samples. Communicator style accounted for approximately 43% of the variation in teacher effectiveness ratings in traditional undergraduate students. However, for the adult learners, teacher communication style accounted for approximately 67% of the variation in teacher effectiveness. These data indicate convincingly that how an instructor communicates with adult learners is very important. To the adult learner, teacher effectiveness means communication effectiveness.

The implication of the above research is clear. The new wave of students entering the college classroom want to interact with their instructors. They want to engage in the educational process with their teachers. Lectures and other noninteractive teaching strategies are not likely to raise students' affective evaluations of their courses or their instructors. To be effective, instructors will need to use teaching strategies that are built on interaction, strategies that use two-way communication for clarifying ideas, influencing attitudes, and solving problems. Discussion groups in particular lend themselves to achieving mastery of subject content and exploring new ideas. Further, faculty need to become sensitive to how they communicate to adults, and to accept and encourage dialogue with students.

The new student has already entered our continuing higher education classrooms. Formal learning is no longer viewed as taking place at a given stage in the human development process. Rather it is "an ongoing condition of existence, inseparable from the quality of life, occupational effectiveness, and responsible citizenship" (Nowlen, 1989, p. 46). The faculty member needs to recognize that teaching is a dynamic endeavor, one that "requires building bridges between the teacher's understanding and the student's learning" (Boyer, 1990, p. 23), and one that requires pedagogical approaches appropriate to a particular student population.

SUMMARY

The new wave of continuing education is challenging institutions of higher education. Our political, economic, social, international, and technological environment is changing. Society is looking to higher education for solutions to the problems faced by our changing world.

Throughout history, universities have responded to change in their environments. Today, social, political, and economic forces call for a new look at the missions of our institutions of higher education, with a greater emphasis on the public service and teaching functions (Boyer, 1990). These changes call for a new organizational structure, in which continuing higher education units provide leadership for the greater academic community. Continuing educators are in a unique position to provide leadership and expertise within their institutions. They may become key players as they provide faculty with new opportunities for teaching, research, and public service.

REFERENCES

Andersen, J. A., Norton, R., & Nussbaum, J. F. (1979, April). *Three investigations exploring relationships among perceived communicator style, perceived teacher immediacy, perceived teacher-student solidarity, teacher effectiveness and student learning.* Paper presented at the annual convention of the American Educational Research Association, San Francisco, CA.

Bloom, B. S. (1976). *Human characteristics and school learning.* New York: McGraw-Hill.

Boyer, E. L. (1990). *Scholarship reconsidered: Priorities of the professoriate.* Princeton, NJ: Carnegie Foundation for the Advancement of Teaching.

Comadena, M. E., & Prusank, D. T. (1988). Communication apprehension and academic achievement among elementary and middle school students. *Communication Education, 37,* 270–277.

Comadena, M. E., Semlak, W. D., Looney, R. E., & Escott, M. E. (1988, May). *Communication apprehension, test anxiety, locus of control as predictors of achievement: A comparative study of traditional students and adult learners.* Paper presented at the annual convention of the International Communication Association, New Orleans, LA.

DeLoughry, T. J. (1991, April 24). Bush proposes "Populist crusade" to reform education. *Chronicle of Higher Education,* pp. A21, A23.

Escott, M. D., Semlak, W. D., & Comadena, M. E. (1989, October). *Faculty attitudes about teaching adult learners at Illinois State University.* Paper presented at the annual conference of National University Continuing Education Association (NUCEA), Region IV, Kalamazoo, MI.

Escott, M. D., Semlak, W. D., & Comadena, M. E. (1990). Communication style and teacher effectiveness: A comparative study of the perceptions of adult learners and traditional undergraduate students. *National Issues in Higher Education, 33,* 109–114.

Knowles, M. S. (1978). *The adult learner: A neglected species* (2nd ed.). Houston: Golf Publishing Company.

Larson, T. D. (1989). New uses for the university. *Educational Record, 70,* 61–65.

Lysakowski, R. S., & Walberg, H. J. (1982). Instructional effects of cues, participation, and corrective feedback: A qualitative synthesis. *American Educational Research Journal, 19,* 559–578.

Norton, R. W. (1977). Teacher effectiveness as a function of communicator style. In B. Ruhen (Ed.), *Communication Yearbook 1* (pp. 525–542). New Brunswick, NJ: Transaction Books.

Norton, R. W. (1978). Foundation of a communicator style construct. *Human Communication Research, 4,* 99–112.

Norton, R. W. (1983). *Communicator style: Theory, applications, and measures.* Beverly Hills, CA: Sage Publications.

Norton, R. W., & Nussbaum, J. F. (1980). Dramatic behaviors of the effective teacher. In D. Nimmo (Ed.), *Communication Yearbook 4* (pp. 565–579). New Brunswick, NJ: Transaction Books.

Nowlen, P. M. (1989). Continuing education: Two perspectives. *Educational Record, 69,* 46–47.

Nussbaum, J. F., Comadena, M. E., & Holladay, S. J. (1987). Classroom verbal behavior of highly effective teachers. *Journal of Thought, 22,* 73–80.

Scott, M. D., & Nussbaum, J. F. (1981). Student perceptions of instructor communication behaviors and their relationship to student evaluation. *Communication Education, 30,* 44–53.

Shinagel, M. (1983). Senior faculty attitudes about teaching evening extension students at Harvard University. *Continuing Higher Education, 31,* 10–12.

Strand, D. (1990). *Continuing education: Defining the missions of AASCU institutions.* American Association of State Colleges and Universities, Washington, D.C.

4   *Research and Continuing Higher Education*

Joe F. Donaldson

Research has become an increasingly important focus within continuing higher education (CHE), as evidenced by a number of activities on the part of continuing higher education's professional associations. Grants to support research are being awarded; preparation of research bibliographies is being supported; and exemplary research is being recognized through award programs. Amid this increased interest, however, questions about research in continuing higher education persist: Who should be conducting the research? What research should be conducted? How does research relate to the practice of continuing education? Finally, how do continuing educators relate to the broader research mission and agendas of their institutions and of the various disciplinary and professional groups with which they work?

The purpose of this chapter is to address these questions by focusing upon continuing education's (CE's) relationship with research, especially on how that relationship is being shaped by changes within higher education and its environment. In exploring these issues, three major points will be addressed. First, more research in continuing education is needed, particularly research that addresses (a) the changes that are being and will be experienced by CHE and (b) the roles and functions that continuing education will be asked to assume in response to these changes. Second, the agenda and function of continuing higher education in the "new wave" era is highly compatible with the research orientation of universities. I will argue that continuing education provides a much-needed bridge between the university and outside individuals, groups, and organizations participating in and having a stake in the research conducted in higher education. Third, the research agenda of continuing higher education and CHE's bridging role in support of the university's research agenda are interdependent.

Both involvement in research and support of it will be required of CHE if it is to achieve its potential in the decade ahead.

TRENDS AND NEEDS IN CONTINUING
HIGHER EDUCATION RESEARCH

Numerous literature reviews of research relating to continuing higher education have been conducted during the past several years. In order to provide a baseline for discussion and to identify areas in special need of future research, I will briefly discuss several of these reviews.

Reviews of Research in Continuing Education

Perhaps the most consistent effort at tracking research in adult and continuing education has been undertaken by Long, who has tracked research appearing in issues of *Adult Education* (now the *Adult Education Quarterly*) from 1964 through 1973 (Long & Agyekum, 1974) and in the proceedings of the Adult Education Research Conference (AERC) from 1971 through 1980 (Long, 1983a), and has summarized a number of research findings in his book *Adult Learning: Research and Practice* (1983b). In these reviews, research is categorized according to research design, topics of research, and contributors and their institutional affiliations. Among the conclusions Long makes are (a) that the amount of research in adult and continuing education is increasing, (b) that most of the research being conducted remains descriptive in nature, and (c) that much research is being conducted in dissertation projects that do not find their way into journals with the frequency one would expect.

In order to classify topics of research in the field, Long developed a 10-topic classification scheme:

1. *Adult development and learning*—theories of learning, adult development, characteristics of adult learners;
2. *Program planning and administration*—initiating and maintaining an educational activity, including the topics of participation, needs assessment, evaluation and program administration;
3. *Institutional sponsors*—sponsors of adult education programs, such as higher education, business and industry, community groups;
4. *Adult education as a field of study*—broad issues related to the "discipline" of adult education and the preparation of professionals;
5. *Instructional materials and methods*—procedures and methods for establishing a relationship between the learner and content, knowledge, or skill;

6. *Philosophical*—rationale and principles of adult education;
7. *Personnel and staff*—human resources needed to develop and deliver adult education;
8. *International*—adult education in countries other than the United States;
9. *Program areas*—special subject matter for particular groups;
10. *Other*—topics different from those in other categories. (Long, 1983a)

Although Long (1983a) found differences in the frequency with which topics were addressed in *Adult Education* and at the Adult Education Research Conference, five topics were addressed most frequently in both: adult development and learning, program planning and administration, adult education as a field of study, instructional materials and methods, and program areas.

A more detailed categorization of literature, a 31-item subject index of articles appearing in *Continuum* (now *Continuing Higher Education Review*) since October 1980, has been developed by Kramer (1984). Kramer undertook this indexing in order to meet the field's need for a systematic delineation of its literature so that this literature would be more useful to researchers, students, and practitioners. According to Kramer, the time had come when the field's leadership would be required to be conversant, through the field's literature and other means, with national practices and approaches. The time had also come when the literature of the field and those who contributed to it would play a new and significant role in shaping the field.

Though not a review of research literature per se, Courtenay's (1990) analysis of adult education administration literature from 1936 through 1989 is also useful, in that it identifies a number of issues related to research and theory in the field, as well as several gaps in that portion of the research literature which addresses the administration of adult education, a particular focus of CHE. By employing (a) an evaluative dimension that focuses on the inclusion in the literature of administrative functions (such as budgeting and leadership) and (b) a descriptive dimension that compares the literature across different adult education practice contexts, Courtenay identifies areas with little data and in need of development. Besides noting that the field's administrative literature is characterized by lack of citation of previous works and heavy dependence on sources outside of adult and continuing education, his analysis raises the central question of whether the administration of adult and continuing education is sufficiently distinctive to warrant separate study and investigation.

More recently Donaldson and Kuhne (1990) have prepared a bibliography of research conducted in continuing higher education from September

1987 through January 1990. Recognizing that reports of research in continuing higher education are scattered throughout a host of publications, the authors attempted to make their bibliography as inclusive as possible. Searches of literature were conducted in the data bases of several fields, including education, health, the social sciences, business, engineering, and the sciences. Members of the National University Continuing Education Association's (NUCEA) Division of Research and departments (and research centers) of adult education, continuing education, and higher education were also surveyed to obtain listings of published research. Contents of journals in the field were likewise reviewed. A total of 212 unduplicated reports of research in various publications were identified through these search procedures.

Although the bibliography was developed using different search criteria than those used by Long (1983a) and by Long and Agyekum (1974), a comparison of the frequency with which research topics were addressed in Long's reviews and in Donaldson and Kuhne's bibliography is instructive. This comparison is illustrated in Table 4.1. For purposes of clarity and comparison, the topic areas of program planning and administration and program areas have been combined into the area of program development, a more abstract category used by Long (1983b) in his book *Adult Learning: Research and Practice*.

The data in Table 4.1 show striking similarities and differences across the three sources with respect to the frequency with which topics have been addressed. According to all three sources, the topic of program development has been considered most frequently, accounting for over 50% of all research reports in the AERC and the bibliography. Subjects considered most frequently within this category in the bibliography include participation and retention of adult learners, needs assessment, and evaluation, and the program area of continuing professional education. The topic of continuing education as a field of study was considered less frequently than in Long's reviews. Although the frequency of occurrence of the instructional material and methods topic does not differ substantially from that reported by Long, the research included in the bibliography focuses primarily on the use of a variety of distance education media and methods for program delivery.

Perhaps as striking as topics that have been considered are those that have not. In the bibliography, the subject of programming for women is considered but once, and no research on equity and cultural pluralism is included. *The Journal of Continuing Higher Education* and *Continuing Higher Education Review* have recently published articles that examine issues related to cultural diversity and describe innovative programs for addressing these issues, but no research articles on these topics have been

Table 4.1 Topics of literature compared across reviews by Long & Agyekum, Long, and Donaldson & Kuhne

Topic	N^a	$\%^a$	N^b	$\%^b$	N^c	$\%^c$
Adult development and learning	21	13.0	43	12	37	17.4
Program development	64	33.5	183	52	118	55.6
Institutional sponsor	5	3.1	25	7	5	2.4
Adult education as a field of study	22	13.7	57	16	12	5.7
Instructional materials and methods	25	15.5	19	5	22	10.4
Philosophical	8	5.0	2	1	8	3.8
Personnel and staff	12	7.5	11	3	10	4.7
International perpective	8	5.0	4	1	0	0
Other	6	3.7	11	3	0	0
Totals	161	100	355	100	212	100

[a]Source: Long & Agyekum, 1974, content of articles in *Adult Education* 1964–1973. The categories of program planning and administration, education of particular groups, and program areas were combined into program development for purposes of comparison.

[b]Source: Long, 1983a, contents of research papers presented at the Adult Education Research Conference, 1971–1980. The categories of program planning and administration and program areas were combined into program development for purposes of comparison.

[c]Source: Donaldson & Kuhne, 1990, content of literature reviewed, September 1987–January 1990.

published. Although there has been no dearth of research on equity and cultural pluralism in leading educational journals, Ross-Gordon (1991) suggests that these topics have yet to garner the attention of researchers in adult education. The same appears to be the case in continuing higher education. In addition, the topic of international perspective, while mentioned in Long's reviews, is glaringly absent in the bibliography. Research in adult and continuing education has been found to lag behind changes and advances in practice (Darkenwald & Merriam, 1982). One hopes that research related to issues of cultural diversity and equity, as well as international issues, will become a more frequent focus of research as the field's research agenda begins to catch up with the changes in practice and programming demanded by issues such as cultural diversity and globalization.

Finally, the administration of organizations of continuing education (in contrast to the administration of program activities) was the topic of only 13 reports (6.1%) included in the bibliography. The infrequency of research reports addressing this level of administration is somewhat surprising, given the greater focus on the organizational level of the CHE administrative literature (Courtenay, 1990). A focus on particular aspects of CE administration and organization will increasingly be needed as CE responds to changes in higher education and in the external organizational environment.

Future Needs

A review of the present state of affairs in continuing higher education research provides only an analysis of what is being done and of deficiencies in the research literature. It is also important to approach this topic from a developmental perspective. Two sources of information indicate what leaders in the field believe to be future research trends. Boyd and Rice (1986) surveyed deans and directors of continuing education at NUCEA member institutions to determine, among other things, what these individuals believed to be topics in most need of research in the field. Responses from 131 deans and directors were grouped into five general categories suggested by Long (1983b). Sixty-three percent of respondents indicated that research was needed in program development; 13% indicated a need in teaching-learning transaction; 8% a need in adult participation and the field of practice and philosophy; and 6% a need for research on the topic of adult learning ability. Boyd and Rice surmise that the interest in program development is due to the relevance to practitioners of the practical nature of research in this area. It is interesting to note that the priority given this perceived need corresponds closely to the priority researchers apparently have given this topic, as evidenced in the frequency with which research reports occur in this category (see Table 4.1).

Using the delphi technique, Long (1990) surveyed 20 deans and directors of continuing higher education about research trends in CHE. Among other questions, they were asked what they considered to be the five topics most in need of research between 1989 and 1998. Ten of the deans/directors responded to all four iterations of the survey. Based upon the findings, Long concluded that

1. Research on learning outcomes was an important concern of respondents, although confusion and disagreement surrounded how to determine the best ways of obtaining the learning outcomes desired; and
2. Educational technology delivery procedures were considered an important area in need of research.

The first topic, learning outcomes, is represented in research conducted within the program development category and is manifested primarily as research on impact evaluation. As noted earlier, the second topic has also already become a focus of some of the research being conducted in CHE.

These two studies provide evidence of (a) some consensus among continuing education leaders about what research should be conducted, and (b) some congruence between topics in need of research and those that are being addressed. However, these findings are only a backdrop against which other trends and issues in the field can be examined as we consider what focus research in continuing higher education might take in the decade ahead. The trends reviewed below do not point to a well-defined future for research in continuing education. In fact, some of the trends are in conflict.

First of all, continuing higher education, like many professions, is increasingly focusing upon the further professionalization of the field. For some, applied and basic research are seen as necessary ingredients in (a) furthering this professionalization, (b) creating a more professional image, and (c) fostering readier acceptance of continuing education by the parent institution as well as by the higher education establishment as a whole. I say "some," because a belief in the importance of research conducted by continuing educators is not necessarily shared by all. Much will depend, therefore, upon how continuing higher education and its leadership view this function over the next several years. This points to the importance of policy at professional and institutional levels: Is research viewed as a useful enterprise and rewarded and supported by the profession, the institution, and the continuing education organization, or is it seen as something that should be done by others and that may get in the way of program and income productivity?

Second, there is a growing readiness to accept context-specific and practice-oriented research. One needs only to look at the work of Schon (1987) and Cervero (1988) on the reflective practitioner and the discussion these works are spawning to see that continuing educators are beginning to focus more upon themselves and the specific context in which they work. Questions about the implicit knowledge that continuing educators use in their work are being raised — for example: What knowledge and behaviors are characteristic of exemplary leaders of continuing education? What mental schema do continuing educators use in their decision-making? What norms and rules that affect administrative actions are inherent in continuing education's subcultures? How can continuing educators and their organizations learn how to learn (higher-order organizational learning)? Continuing educators have always prided themselves on effectively executing the boundary-spanning role in their institutions. Although some research has been done in this area (e.g., Smutz, 1985; Brown, 1985; Damron, 1986), we know very little about the knowledge and behavior of those continuing educators who perform this role in exemplary fashion. As was noted in Chapter Two, this area of research will become increasingly important as cultures suffuse and bridges between the university and its various publics become more critical to institutional survival and functioning. So too will studies that explore interorganizational relationships between continuing education organizations and other types of organizations (e.g., professional associations, business and industry, community groups, governmental agencies).

This category of research also focuses on what continuing educators actually do in their work. Four major approaches to gaining this understanding have been nurtured in recent years. In the descriptive approach, continuing educators are defined and described with respect to their demographic characteristics, prior experience, career aspirations, and personal traits (e.g., NUCEA, 1990; Freedman, 1987). In the functions and role approach, questions related to general functions and roles of all continuing educators as well as those in particular continuing education positions (e.g., dean, conference director) are explored, often in relation to some other variable(s) of interest (e.g., Brown, 1985; Brue, 1990). In the behavioral approach, the object of research is to detail through direct observation or self-reports the characteristics of continuing educators' work and the roles they perform (e.g., Griggs & Morgan, 1988; Donaldson, 1989). The proficiency approach focuses on the general and position-specific competencies continuing educators must have in order to function effectively in their jobs. The development of proficiencies as part of the NUCEA Continuing Higher Education Leadership Project is an example of this approach (Knox, 1987).

Although work in this area has begun to increase, additional research is needed if continuing educators are to understand the subtleties of their work and build professional development strategies that address the realities they face. Work in this area also points to the need for a more differentiated understanding of different roles in continuing higher education. Much of the prescriptive literature addresses the work of continuing educators as if they performed a homogeneous set of roles. However, findings from several studies within this category of research (e.g., Brown, 1985; Damron, 1986; Donaldson, 1989) point to the need for research on specific roles and for meta-analyses that compare and contrast various CHE roles and the institutional and programmatic contexts in which they are performed. Research in this area will also contribute to answering the question that has been raised by Courtenay's (1990) analysis of the field's administration literature. Is administration of the field distinctive enough to warrant separate study and research?

Third, the larger research community is increasingly disposed to accept local and contextually based research. This is especially true in education and in the areas of organizational and management theory. Recent qualitative research on organizational culture and leadership are but two examples of this shift in focus. The force of the positivistic research paradigm is being counterbalanced by increased acceptance of postpositivistic paradigms (Lincoln & Guba, 1985). Although adult education research was at one time becoming increasingly quantitative (Matkin, 1979), more and more qualitative research is being accepted for publication in leading journals of the field. For example, several recent issues of the *Adult Education Quarterly* contain reports of research that have been conducted using postpositivistic paradigms. This trend opens avenues to research at the local level and to its publication that have been unavailable until now. Tied to this trend is the recognition that generalizations from large-scale survey research are perhaps not as useful to practice as was once thought. Several recent studies (e.g., Graham, 1988), for example, have uncovered trends at particular institutions that are at odds with some generalizations that have been accepted for years. Although large-scale studies provide broad perspectives on and generalizations about the field, local studies often serve local decision-making as well as, and in some cases better than, the large-scale studies to which the field has looked for assistance in the past.

Fourth, as society's cultures suffuse, continuing educators must begin to focus on ways to program for, market to, recruit, and retain diverse ethnic and minority learners. As was noted earlier, research in this critically important area is severely lacking. If continuing education is to respond to the needs and interests of racial and ethnic minority groups, much more research will have to be conducted in this and related areas. Ross-Gordon (1991) suggests several research questions that might be considered in this area. For example,

- "What characteristics are observed in the program planning and implementation processes used by organizations which effectively serve minority adults?" (p. 8)
- "What forms of outreach/marketing are most successful with specific minority clientele?" (p. 8)
- "What types of educational programs are most effective in changing awareness levels of adult education staff regarding the particular needs of and approaches useful with minority adults?" (p. 9)

Fifth, outcome and impact studies are being developed and conducted by institutions of higher education to improve local decision-making, to improve the recruitment and retention of the more limited pool of students, and to respond to our society's growing demand for educational accountability (Donaldson, 1990). As noted earlier, deans and directors of continuing education have identified this topic as one which will be important between 1989 and 1998 (Long, 1990). Similar studies will need to be undertaken for similar purposes in continuing higher education. Failure to do so will limit the field's ability to recruit and retain students and its knowledge of program impact.

Sixth, the focus on strategic planning in higher education and in continuing education (Simerly & Associates, 1987), coupled with further development of environmental scanning techniques (Simpson, 1990), provide opportunities for a better understanding of institutional environments. If continuing higher education is to serve as a major bridging mechanism for the university, continued research in this area is also needed. As continuing education's and higher education's external environment becomes ever more heterogeneous and more uncertain, more sophisticated methods for understanding that environment will be required.

Finally, adults are returning to undergraduate and graduate study in growing numbers. This phenomenon has drawn the attention of administrators and faculty members across the campus. Research and large-scale studies of this phenomenon and its implications for higher education are being conducted in fields outside of adult and continuing education. This trend raises a new question: Are continuing educators in the ironic position of protecting not only their administrative "turf," but their research turf as well, or is this a turf to be shared with all? Another prediction of deans and directors in Long's (1990) delphi study was that "research and development is not likely to be done by individuals specifically associated with continuing higher education units and/or funded for that purpose" (p. 9). The coming of a "new wave" era raises important research and strategic questions about the role of continuing education in areas of continuing education research that until recently did not particularly interest anyone else in the academy.

The literature reviewed and the discussion of trends not only have identified areas in need of further research in CHE, but have also raised a number of questions and highlighted several issues. How these questions will be answered and how these issues will be resolved is difficult to predict. Continuing educators' focus on research has only recently begun to reach a critical level, and little is still known about the role that research will play in the field in the years ahead. What we do know is that those who have reviewed the field's literature point to continuing educators' growing recognition of the importance of research. However, we also know that barriers exist to continuing educators' involvement in research. Some of these barriers are a lack of time, a yearning for the days when less was expected of continuing educators in the research arena (Boyd & Rice, 1986), a lack of research divisions and capacity within continuing education organizations (Boyd & Rice, 1986), and pessimism about obtaining the funding required to conduct the research that is needed (Long, 1990). The opportunities for involvement in research, as well as the barriers to involvement, raise major policy issues for the field at both professional and institutional levels. As Long (1990) notes, however, the leadership of continuing education will have to assume greater responsibility for developing mechanisms for research and development if research is to become an integral part of continuing educators' roles. This means that chief executive officers of continuing education units will have to accept research as a value within their units, along with the values of program creativity and productivity, if research and writing among practitioners are to be nurtured. But a focus on continuing education's bridging function will also be required in the new era we are entering.

RESEARCH AND CONTINUING EDUCATION'S BRIDGING FUNCTION

The role of knowledge in society is changing. Not only are we becoming an information society, but information derived from research is increasingly being called upon to solve complex local, national, and global problems. This trend is requiring higher education to focus on both basic and applied research. As Lynton and Elman (1987) note, A. D. Bromley, and eminent nuclear physicist, has made this point quite forcefully:

> Using Vannevar Bush's image of science as the endless frontier, he pointed out that science has both external and internal frontiers. The internal frontiers are "those where human knowledge is pushing most vigorously toward the unknown." The external frontiers, characterized as "no less important," are those that border on the many areas of applications of science: "the federal government, the educational establishment, the private sector, national security and defense, world science and technology, the developing world, and U.S. society itself." (Bromley, 1982, p. 1035, cited in Lynton & Elman, 1987, pp. 22–23)

As higher education moves into the future, continuing educators have the opportunity to contribute in meaningful ways to science's frontiers.

However, just as barriers exist to continuing educators' involvement in research, so too do barriers exist to continuing education's support of higher education's research function. One barrier, which has just been discussed, is continuing educators' lack of involvement in research. Although a great deal of research is being conducted in continuing higher education and interest in research is mounting, an increased focus on research and an understanding of the research process do not pervade the field. According to Campbell (1984), continuing educators have tended to focus on advancement of the field through political and economic tactics rather than through systematic inquiry. He goes on to note that what is required in the field is a deliberate shift from the "entrepreneurial-administrative-marketing" work model, or what Siegel (1989) calls continuing education's "paradigm of practice obsession," to a "professional-academic" model consistent with the university's emerging responsibilities in continuing education. Many continuing educators, lacking experience in research and not understanding the research process or the value research has in and for their own practice, feel alienated from researchers and blame research for interfering with the accomplishment of continuing education's programming agenda. As a result, many fail to perceive involvement in research as an opportunity to move closer to the academic mainstream and strengthen CE's relationship to the university's research function (Donaldson, 1990).

Although overcoming the barrier of involvement is a necessary condition for fuller support of research by CE, it is by itself insufficient. Another barrier must also be addressed. This barrier is the perception by the academy that continuing education has little to offer in regard to research support. Matkin (1990) notes in reference to technology transfer, for example, that "often CE's capabilities as an agent of technology transfer are not recognized either by the faculty or the administration of the university" (p. 221). This lack of recognition of what is being done and what could be done by CE results in CE's being bypassed as an appropriate contributor to higher education's research agendas on the campus. Its contribution and its potential are insufficiently appreciated in the literature as well (see, e.g., Lynton & Elman, 1987).

As was noted in Chapter Two, much of this lack of recognition is tied to continuing education's need to act as a more effective bridge between academic units and the external groups upon which the academy depends to carry out the research function. But, as Matkin (1990) notes, the role of continuing education is being broadened and redefined:

> This broadening of the definition of CE to include activities beyond classroom instruction indicates that the role of CE is in the process of being reconceptualized in American research universities. This reconceptualization is part of a general pattern of change that includes the new emphasis on technology transfer, relations with industry, and serving university graduates after they have their degrees. (p. 233)

Many institutions are recognizing that continuing education's current contacts, client service orientation,and administrative policies and procedures can serve them well in technology and knowledge transfer activities (Matkin, 1990). Continuing education can provide a much-needed bridge between the university and (a) consumers of university-based research,

(b) individuals and groups that need to have problems researched, (c) researchers in industry, government, and the not-for-profit sector with whom faculty can collaborate, (d) audiences that can help to locate research funding and research opportunities, and (e) opinion leaders and opinion-makers who can make resources and populations more accessible to university researchers. It will be up to continuing education, however, to participate strategically in policy deliberations that contribute to the reconceptualization and broadening of its mission to include this bridging function, and to employ strategies that enable it to play a more central role in research.

Strategies that can be employed to support the institution's research function fall within three broad functional categories, as identified by Lynton and Elman (1987):

1. Information and communication;
2. Initiation; and
3. Brokering and negotiating.

Information and Communication

Lynton and Elman (1987) define the information and communication function as giving "potential clients information about pertinent resources of the university, inform[ing] faculty of external demands and opportunities, and effect[ing] the proper match between external needs and internal expertise" (p. 33). This definition captures the information processing, external representation, and communication roles continuing educators have traditionally played in programming. In the new wave era, however, they will need to extend this boundary-spanning role to include a focus upon the institution's research mission. Resources represented to client groups will include research as well as instruction. Faculty will be informed of research as well as programmatic opportunities. And the continuing educator will be responsible for facilitating the matching of external research needs and internal research expertise.

The addition of the research focus to the continuing educator's role will, however, require continuing educators to shed their apprehensions about research and engage in research themselves. It will require attention to both professional and ethnic cross-cultural perspectives so that information sharing and communication are sensitive and effective. These adjustments will be required by the changing nature of the work force (Ehrlich & Garland, 1988) and the suffusion of professional cultures. Perhaps most important, however, will be the action of continuing education's leadership to grasp this opportunity and support research in ways not previously considered appropriate. Such a change in focus will be essential to the long-term survival of continuing education units as distinct organizational sub-units of the parent organization. Unless CE participates in and contributes to higher education's increased emphasis on technology and knowledge transfer, on developing partnerships with business, professional associations, governmental agencies and other organizations, and on fostering the economic development of communities, states, and regions, CE will probably become increasingly marginal to the parent institution (Votruba, 1987). Many of the contributions CE can make will come in the form of information processing and communications. Still others will be made in the functional category of initiation.

Initiation

In the initiation category, CE takes action to initiate and/or support research activities of faculty. This research may focus on CE topics and intersect with interests of the CHE unit, or it may be totally unrelated to CE. Actions which can be taken in the initiation category include the following:

1. *Developing projects that include a research component.* Innovative programs or means of delivery can include an applied research or evaluation component in which faculty members can participate. Funded projects can be designed to include applied research components or provide a basis for conducting basic research. Furthermore, basic research can be built into applied-research projects, such as evaluations and needs assessments.

2. *Supporting faculty research directly and indirectly,* especially research that is of particular interest to the continuing education unit or is related to the unit's work with particular client groups. Research can be encouraged by providing faculty members with examples of ways they can conduct research related to their participation in CE programs. Topics could include the instructional effectiveness of various distance education technologies, work with learners from diverse cultures, and the administration of continuing education itself. In-kind support of faculty research can be provided through such means as providing institutional data and clerical support and supporting the development of publications (proceedings, articles, and monographs, and even books) that may arise out of faculty members' participation in CE programs. Administrators can participate in team research projects with faculty members, thereby supporting faculty research by providing time and expertise. Lastly, CE can set aside funding to directly support the research of faculty. The more this funding is distributed on a competitive basis through peer review and receives support from appropriate academic units, the more will CE's contribution in this area be recognized (Donaldson, 1990).

3. *Developing and managing interdisciplinary research projects.* By virtue of its work with multiple campus disciplines and professions, CE is in a unique position to facilitate research that cuts across disciplinary and professional boundaries. This is particularly true of continuing education for the professions, where issues and questions common to the education of this group of adults can be approached from a comparative perspective.

4. *Sponsoring national and international conferences, seminars, and symposia that focus on faculty research.* Matkin (1990) notes, for example, that continuing educators at Stanford, the Massachusetts Institute of Technology, the University of California at Berkeley, and the Pennsylvania State University actively supported technology and knowledge transfer by convening conferences, disseminating research results, providing background information, and presenting programs on technical subjects for nontechnical people.

Although these initiation strategies take continuing education beyond simply processing information and communicating about research opportunities, yet another function must be performed in order for continuing education to contribute as fully as possible to research. This function is the actual linking of researchers to resources, and it requires a focus on brokering and negotiating.

Brokering and Negotiating

Brokering and negotiating strategies include creating opportunities for faculty to collaborate with nonuniversity professionals in activities that can lead to identification of (a) research problems, (b) funding sources to support research, and (c) collaborative research projects with these nonuniversity professionals. These strategies also include matching faculty research projects with research in government, industry, and business. The functions of brokering and negotiating are not unfamiliar to most continuing educators, especially those who have had experience in developing contract programs with a variety of other organizations. As continuing education's role is reconceptualized and broadened, however, these functions will have to be expanded into the research domain.

Continuing educators' success in brokering and negotiating effectively will depend not only upon their skills in these two areas, but also on their understanding of the development and maintenance of temporary boundary transaction systems (Adams, 1976) within which brokering and negotiating operate. All interorganizational arrangements, whether programmatic or research-related, require the development of a temporary organization or system between cooperating organizations. Temporary organizations formed between different types of organizations (for example, university-business partnerships) are cross-cultural. In addition, authority within the system is decentralized; there are multiple decision centers; and policies and procedures are fluid (Goodman, 1981). Continuing educators must therefore be able to manage not only tasks but also the system in which those tasks are performed. This will require them to be aware of, understand, and assume several additional roles. They must be communication facilitators, ensuring that individuals within the system are not only communicating but understanding each other. They must be "underground" managers, making sure that tasks within the system are performed, but doing so subtly and often indirectly. They must be system negotiators, working to negotiate an order for the temporary system different from the order in their own institution and the organization with which their institution is working. And they must be shuttle diplomats, working between organizations to gather and transmit information and work out any conflicts that may arise (Bennis & Slater, 1968). These additional roles must be performed, and performed well, by continuing educators if they are to play their part within the strategic function of research brokering and negotiating that is required by CE's redefined and broadened function.

INVOLVEMENT IN AND SUPPORT OF RESEARCH

Research has become an increasingly important focus within continuing education. That focus must continue to be nurtured if continuing educators' involvement in research is to expand. From the literature and an examination of trends, a few critical areas have been identified in which research will be needed in the coming decade. Several roles that continuing education can play, and in fact must play, in supporting the research function in higher education have also been identified. The areas emphasized as requiring additional research in CHE, the recommended increased involvement of continuing educators in research, and needed support of continuing education as part of the institution's research mission are not only highly compatible goals, but interdependent ones.

Several areas of compatibility illustrate the interdependence of research involvement and support by CE. For example, continuing educators can best perform brokering and negotiating and information and communication functions when they understand fully the boundary-spanning roles and operations of their units and the knowledge and behaviors of continuing education's exemplary boundary spanners. This is an area in need of additional research and one where continuing education practice will be put to the test by higher education. In addition, because continuing education is at the boundary of the institution and spans that boundary, organizations of continuing education provide a unique focus for research (Devlin, 1982). To date, continuing education has not fully capitalized on that unique focus to make contributions to its knowledge base and to the effectiveness of practice. Likewise, to be effective environmental information processors, continuing educators will need to know what environmental scanning techniques are most effective and to test increasingly sophisticated techniques for scanning their environments.

It will also be important to assess the impact not only of educational programs, but of research bridging mechanisms as well, if continuing education is to demonstrate its efficacy to internal and external stakeholders alike. The broadening and reconceptualization of CE's role will bring increased examination and assessment of organizations of continuing education (Matkin, 1990). The long range impact of CE activities, another area in need of further research, will therefore also become a consideration in the research of the "new wave" era.

We need a better understanding of the recruitment and retention of currently underserved client groups (including racial and ethnic minorities), of their participation patterns, and of the characteristics of programs that nurture cultural diversity among CE staff and within CE programs if continuing education is to be an effective mirror for the parent institution, capturing the institution's environment in all its complexity and richness. This too is an area in which continuing education's involvement in and support of research is essential.

Finally, continuing education units can be recognized as important stakeholders in and contributors to the university's research mission only if they are viewed as units that (a) support the research missions of their institutions *and* (b) explore the internal and external frontiers of their own art and science.

REFERENCES

Adams, J. S. (1976). The structure and dynamics of behavior in organizational boundary roles. In M. D. Dunnette (Ed.), *Handbook of industrial and organizational psychology* (pp. 1175–1199). Chicago: Rand McNally.

Bennis, W. G., & Slater, P. E. (1968). *The temporary society*. New York: Harper & Row.

Boyd, R. H., & Rice, D. (1986). An overview of research activity in adult and continuing education. *Continuum, 50*(1), 37–46.

Bromley, A. D. (1982). The other frontiers of science. *Science, 215*, 1035.

Brown, C. E. (1985). *The relationship between latent social role orientation and boundary role behavior of deans of continuing education in private research universities*. Unpublished doctoral dissertation, Syracuse University.

Brue, D. (1990). Perceived occupational needs and job fulfillment in continuing higher education: A comparative analysis by level of employment. In *Proceedings of the 31st Annual Adult Education Research Conference* (pp. 37–42). Athens, GA: AERC (no copyright).

Campbell, D. D. (1984). *The new majority: Adult learners in the university.* Edmonton, Alberta, Canada: University of Alberta Press.

Cervero, R. M. (1988). *Effective continuing education for professionals.* San Francisco: Jossey-Bass.

Courtenay, B. C. (1990). An analysis of adult education administration literature, 1936–1989. *Adult Education Quarterly, 40*(2), 63–74.

Damron, M. R. (1986). *Boundary spanning in highly institutionalized environments: Continuing higher education – extension administrators.* Unpublished doctoral dissertation, University of Missouri–St. Louis.

Darkenwald, G. G., & Merriam, S. B. (1982). *Adult education: Foundations of Practice.* New York: Harper & Row.

Devlin, L. E. (1982). Marginality: Some conceptual approaches for university extension. *Canadian Journal of University Continuing Education, 8*(2), 4–9.

Donaldson, J. F. (1989, October). *Continuing education administrators' work and working roles.* Paper presented at the annual conference of the American Association for adult and continuing education, Atlantic City, NJ.

Donaldson, J. F. (1990). *Managing credit programs in continuing higher education.* Urbana, IL: University of Illinois.

Donaldson, J. F., & Kuhne, G. W. (1990). *Bibliography of research in continuing higher education with a compendium of contributed abstracts, September 1987 through January 1990.* Washington, DC: National University Continuing Education Association.

Ehrlich, L. F., & Garland, S. B. (1988, September 19). For American business, a new world of workers. *Business Week,* pp. 112–120.

Freedman, L. (1987). *Quality in continuing education.* San Francisco: Jossey-Bass.

Goodman, R. A. (1981). *Temporary systems: Professional development, manpower utilization, task effectiveness and innovation.* New York: Praeger.

Graham, S. (1988). The needs and learning preferences of community college adults: Implications for program planning and marketing. *Community College Review, 15*(3), 41–47.

Griggs, K., & Morgan, S. D. (1988). What are the administrative tasks and priorities for continuing education administrators? *Journal of Continuing Higher Education, 36*(2), 6–10.

Knox, A. B. (1987). Leadership challenges to continuing higher education. *Journal of Higher Education Management, 2*(2), 1–14.

Kramer, J. L. (1984). The literature of continuing education. *Continuum, 48*(2), 231–270.

Lincoln, Y. S., & Guba, E. G. (1985). *Naturalistic inquiry.* Newbury Park, CA: Sage.

Long, H. B. (1983a). Characteristics of adult education research reported at the adult education research conference, 1971–1980. *Adult Education, 33*(2), 79–96.

Long, H. B. (1983b). *Adult learning: Research and practice.* New York: Cambridge University Press.

Long, H. B. (1990). Research trends, topics, results, approaches and funding in continuing higher education, 1989-1998: A delphi study. *Continuing Higher Education Review, 54*(1), 1-10.

Long, H. B., & Agyekum, S. K. (1974). *Adult Education* 1964-1973: Reflections of a changing discipline. *Adult Education, 24*(2), 99-120.

Lynton, E. A., & Elman, S. E. (1987). *New priorities for the university: Meeting society's needs for applied knowledge and competent individuals.* San Francisco: Jossey-Bass.

Matkin, G. W. (1979). Theory, method, and appropriateness in adult education research. In *Proceedings of the 21st Adult Education Research Conference* (pp. 138-143). Vancouver, British Columbia, Canada.

Matkin, G. W. (1990). *Technology transfer and the university.* New York: Macmillan.

National University Continuing Education Association (1990). The "Next Generation" Survey – 1990. Washington, DC: Author.

Ross-Gordon, J. M. (1991). Needed: A multicultural perspective for adult education research. *Adult Education Quarterly, 42*(1), 1-16.

Schon, D. A. (1987). *Educating the reflective practitioner.* San Francisco: Jossey-Bass.

Siegel, B. L. (1989, April). *Long on management; short on soul?* Presentation made at the National University Continuing Education Association Conference, Salt Lake City, UT.

Simerly, R. G., & Associates. (1987). *Strategic planning and leadership in continuing education.* San Francisco: Jossey-Bass.

Simpson, E. (1990). Keeping pace with changing societal trends. In *A Handbook for professional developing in continuing higher education* (pp. 101-105). Washington, DC: National University Continuing Education Association.

Smutz, W. D. (1985, March). *Differential performance of formal boundary spanners in the formation of university/professional association interorganizational relationships.* Paper presented at the Annual Meeting of the Association for the Study of Higher Education, Chicago, IL.

Votruba, J. C. (1987). From marginality to mainstream: Strategies for increasing internal support for continuing education. In R. G. Simerly & Associates, *Strategic planning and leadership in continuing education* (pp. 185-201). San Francisco: Jossey-Bass.

5 Organizational Structure and Performance Dynamics in Continuing Education Administration

B. Kay King
Allan W. Lerner

Since the mid-1950s, there has been continuous discussion about the ideal administrative model for continuing education (CE). While this discussion has sometimes lapsed into the perennial debate over "centralization versus decentralization," it has also resulted in some degree of consensus on certain points. One such idea might be summarized as the following general principle: The best administrative structure for continuing education is the one that will best allow continuing education to serve the mission and priorities of the parent institution. The great virtue of this principle is that it discourages the futile search for "the one best way," a search that organization theory and public administration gave up some time ago.

While this principle from the professionals' current conventional wisdom is an advance over past intransigence as well as past fads, it also implies that there is a prerequisite for success in continuing education development: If the ideal structure for continuing education is that which conforms to the parent institution's mission and priorities, then the parent

Previously published as "Organizational Structure and Performance Dynamics in Continuing Education Administration" by B. Kay King and Allan W. Lerner, 1987, *Continuing Higher Education Review, 3*, pp. 21–38. Copyright 1987 by National University Continuing Education Association (NUCEA). Adapted by permission. Referencing and footnoting have been changed to correspond with the format of this volume. Order of authorship is alphabetical.

institution must have a clear idea of its mission and priorities especially in the continuing education domain, if continuing education units are to function at maximum effectiveness.

It is true in one sense that there are as many missions and priorities for continuing education as there are universities. All the same, we believe that, overall, two dimensions emerge regarding universities' expectations for continuing education units: Either continuing education units are expected to be aggressive profit centers, or they are expected to be conventional academic units that happen to have an external student clientele. Furthermore, the modern, large, complex university often melds these distinct expectations to varying degrees, so that now continuing education units are often expected to meet both descriptions.

The purpose of this chapter is to probe the nature of this dual expectation and the stresses and possibilities it can create. The dual conception of the continuing education unit might be judged by some to be schizophrenic or, at best, suspiciously hybrid. We believe that the dual expectation climate is likely to become more and more prevalent. Without clinging to an inappropriate optimism, and drawing instead on a careful conceptualization of the underlying organizational dynamics, it would appear that the dual expectation framework can be accommodated in a well-integrated model for continuing education in the context of the modern, large university.

A major theme of this chapter, however, is that if the integrated model is to flourish, its structure as a third alternative must be understood. This in turn requires a fuller grasp of the two pure types, which are equally viable alternatives. A comparison of the two pure types indicates how specific elements of each must be combined to produce the integrated model. Our goal is not to argue for any one of these models — the entrepreneurial, the academic, or the integrated. Rather, we endeavor to explicate the organizational goals and purposes of each model, and to identify the structural and value issues underlying the proper operation of each, as well as the corresponding trade-offs. Only thus do policy and structural choices become goal-driven rather than rationalized by institutional default.

Continuing educational units suffering such conditions may be doomed to evaluation according to inappropriate and jumbled criteria, evaluation that produces equally irrelevant praise and criticism. Perhaps worse, such units may not have a clear understanding of their own responsibilities, for lack of a clearly communicated expectation from the larger organization. With vague, contradictory, and oscillating signals as to how the continuing education unit should be integrated with other activities (e.g., teaching, research, recruitment of qualified students, solicitation of capital funding), it may be forced into de facto isolation from the larger organization. A unit in such circumstances is not positioned to effectively further the goals of the parent institution. A clearer understanding of our alternate models for continuing education unit configuration is a prerequisite not only for the continuing education unit to function satisfactorily, but for the larger institution and its environment (i.e., faculty, administrators, other organizational units, students, and external audiences) to make full use of continuing education capabilities. With this perspective in mind, we turn to a consideration of each of the continuing education unit models we have identified.

THE ENTREPRENEURIAL MODEL

General Unit Orientation

The major goal in the entrepreneurial model is to make money. The resultant emphasis is on rendering the continuing education units self-supporting and also capable of providing funds to the parent institution. The entrepreneurial organization tends to be run as a small business within the framework of a loosely coupled larger organization (Wieck, 1978). The unit emphasizes cost efficiency. In its administrative style and internal unit culture, it emulates the external corporate business world. Examples of this may include everything from high-tech office communications systems to the "dress for success" look for the staff, well-appointed conference spaces, and all the amenities typical of a successful corporate enterprise. Decisions about programming are based on the bottom line. Contracts are commonplace. Opportunities to deliver "public service programs" are of only secondary importance and tend to be sought out only if they are tied to the prospects of earning money through grants associated with such programs.

General Pattern of Unit Configuration

Because the entrepreneurial model places a premium on aggressive, profitable contract capture, it stresses the marketing function and is structurally elaborated and well developed to perform this function. Subroutines are developed and personnel are organized around the performance of marketing functions. Through specific titles combined into subunits, the unit is developed to sustain and demystify the marketing process. A full-time staff of "field coordinators" functions as a sales force armed with a well-developed list of available programs. Such persons are key "boundary" actors (Wilensky, 1967). They link the unit and, through it, the university to an external clientele defined as a market.

Criteria for Success

In the entrepreneurial model, success is measured incrementally, in dollars. The better the bottom line, the greater the success of the unit.

Disadvantages of the Entrepreneurial Model

Although the entrepreneurial continuing education unit tends to be seen as an entrepreneurial island in a nonprofit archipelago, it is still highly sensitive to the level of appropriations committed to it by the parent institution. This is especially true in the initial stages of unit growth, when the critical mass must be created that is needed to develop a unit capable of capturing a portion of the market sufficient to generate profit. The frequent organizational tendency to fund even entrepreneurism "on the cheap" makes such units especially vulnerable to undercapitalization amid entrepreneurial rhetoric. Similarly, to the extent that intra-unit office staffing, procurement, and general management are constrained by public or nonprofit-sector legal, contractual, and customary practices, the overhead control and related administrative constraints may distress the entrepreneurial unit in its attempt to be "lean and mean."

In the parent institution generally, faculty are not rewarded for the amount of money they can generate with their course and workshop offerings. More commonly their incentives are tied to the amount of research dollars they generate, the peer-evaluated quality of their research, and, to varying degrees, student receptivity to their teaching. Generally, frequent continuing education activity is categorized as "public service" and is a function of minor import in career performance evaluation. Remuneration for such service tends to be perceived as consulting profits, and indulgence in such activity may be perceived as an indication of unscholarly priorities, a negative assessment compounded by resentment of the added income a colleague earns for teaching in continuing education.

As a result, continuing education units on the entrepreneurial model may encounter senior and junior faculty resistance. The unit's alienation from faculty may be compounded by the resulting pressure on the entrepreneurial unit manager to recruit faculty outside the parent institution. This raises the prospect of a self-fulfilling prophecy of faculty alienation from continuing education at worst, and a lack of faculty support for unit goals and interests at best.

The entrepreneurial continuing education unit often risks being at odds with the prevailing administrative style of the parent institution. The unit is designed to be an efficient, aggressive, highly responsive unit within the context of a larger institution more likely to operate with an admixture of traditional academic values, a bureaucratic ethos, and a tradition of considerable faculty autonomy. The continuing education unit must span the bureaucratic culture of offices of admissions and records and business offices on the one hand, and departments governed by majority vote in faculty meetings on the other. This creates a dual pressure on the entrepreneurial unit, a tendency to "vertical integration." The entrepreneurial unit is thereby predisposed to attempt to absorb bureaucratic functions within its own structural arrangements — for example, by establishing its own business office. Otherwise its ability to control the speed, style, and aptness of its response to its market will be reduced. Similarly, the desire to deal administratively with an "executive in charge" at the faculty level can create an illusion of central academic planning at the faculty level, and at worst can contribute to political tensions with departments and colleges.

The continuing education unit on the entrepreneurial model faces further difficulties in the realm of academic strategic planning. Because of the academic aspect of the tendency to vertical integration discussed above, the entrepreneurial continuing education unit is limited in its ability to develop long-range plans and commitments for program delivery and assured resource and faculty availability. Curriculum review committees to help ensure the quality of programming and instruction are not administratively accountable to the unit. It can be seriously disadvantaged in its ability to secure long-term contractual relationships and to follow through on commitments elicited in earlier negotiating stages with clients.

Advantages

The entrepreneurial model offers a genuine opportunity to generate income. It offers the prospect of new money for the parent university — money that can help support perennially underfunded needs, including graduate student support, research support, and funds for the development of new programs. Furthermore, the entrepreneurial unit can be an unambiguous measure of success. Performance is evaluated in terms that can be easily understood by faculty and administration: dollars, enrollment, and number of programs.

The entrepreneurial model is also highly compatible with the values of the marketplace. The more the continuing education unit is organized and evaluated like a business, the more trustworthy it becomes to its clients in the external environment. The unit need no longer appeal for tolerance of the peculiarities of academia. Other large-scale formal organizations understand bottom-line and marketing issues. The continuing education unit now exhibits a structure and set of priorities with which these external actors are familiar.

The entrepreneurial organization also controls its own fate. The greater the unit's power to make decisions regarding program offerings, hiring of faculty, payment of faculty, and devising contractual arrangements without being constrained by university bylaws and regulations written for conventional units, the greater its ability to articulate and pursue an agenda. The unit can act with the autonomy necessary to react to its market.

Having described the entrepreneurial model and its advantages and disadvantages, we now turn to the academic model.

THE ACADEMIC MODEL

General Unit Orientation

The academic model in its pure form tends to treat the continuing education unit as an academic unit—if not as a department, then as an academic "program" drawing faculty from contributing departmental units. As a result, the unit's goals, like the goals of academic departments and programs, are multiple and operationally somewhat vague. They reflect the working priorities of a conventional department or program: research, teaching, and public service.

General Pattern of Unit Configuration

Because the continuing education unit on the academic model must meet the general obligations of a department, it has, for better or worse, the administrative configuration of a conventional department or program, which is designed to further a conventional academic unit's activities. Its administrators must place a premium on staff offerings that fit the teaching and research interests of faculty, which are usually articulated through their department and program head. The latters' cooperation understandably depends on the compatibility of continuing education interests with the agenda of the departments from which faculty are drawn, and with the professional interests of the departments and their faculty.

The continuing education unit in the academic model focuses inward more than it does in the entrepreneurial model. This is because its day-today environment consists of the pressures and institutional politics of academic departments and their respective colleges. The emphasis is on structures for working with appropriate faculty and/or with the executive officers of departments and colleges to obtain permission to undertake arrangements with such faculty.

In this model the continuing education administrator's role is that of tactful broker of interests in an internal service position, rather than that of an aggressive boundary actor. Pursuit of external contacts takes second place to working with internal units or with faculty deputized for such discussion. Within this framework, the continuing education unit may adopt a service posture or a co-developer posture. The choice of emphasis would most likely depend on whether given departments are hierarchically organized, with strong executives, or are democratic/consensual in structure, or are populated by prominent senior faculty enjoying considerable autonomy and interested in direct contact with the continuing education unit.

Offices will tend to physically resemble departmental offices; a corporate ambiance would be disdained.

Criteria for Success

In principle the criteria for success are the same as those for any academic unit on campus — research, securing research grants, achieving excellence in teaching, and providing public service. However, as the ratio of genuine attention and lip service devoted to each of these criteria varies from institution to institution, the actual criteria applied to the continuing education unit may vary as well.

Generally speaking, the continuing education unit in the academic model will fare well within its institution to the degree that it is able to demonstrate success according to those criteria valued most highly by its parent institution. Thus, a continuing education unit at a university emphasizing research and teaching will do best if it secures the participation of influential faculty whose credentials will impress researchers in client relationships fashioned through continuing education activity. Failing that, if the unit emphasizes quality teaching at an institution that stresses research but also cares about good teaching, the continuing education unit may rattle along in a safe but decidedly secondary category of esteem, resource allocation, and institutional visibility.

The continuing education unit on the academic model is funded through the same processes as any other academic unit or department. It must make its case for funding like any other unit at its parent institution.

Disadvantages

The continuing education unit on the academic model must participate in the fratricidal competition among units at the parent institution. The unit may often find itself in the politically sensitive situation of competing with other academic units for faculty time, departmental resources, and jurisdictional legitimacy. Also, depending upon the degree to which particular departments have developed traditions for autonomous disciplinary extension programs, administrative structures for continuing education can develop within other academic units. Parallel support service units can also develop within each of the colleges. This can further exacerbate the jurisdictional problem for the unit (Lerner, November, 1986). In the academic model, support for the continuing education unit is provided through the funding process governing departments and colleges in general. Therefore, in contrast to the entrepreneurial model, depending on the particular leadership at any given time, continuing education funding levels may vary independent of the unit's performance.

A further disadvantage facing units on this model is the fact that the maze of university structure, which often appears counterintuitive to those in the private sector, can discourage external constituencies from contacting the unit. Academic professionals tend to underestimate the opaqueness of university structure and procedures to the eyes of outsiders. As a conventional academic unit, the continuing education unit is no longer the sole focus — and arguably not even the most obvious starting point — for inquiries and contacts from outside. The conventional university process of consultation and committee consensus-building often inadvertently gives an impression of ambivalence and vacillation to external parties awaiting responses from the university regarding program offerings. At a minimum, the process can become an unintended obstacle in attempting to establish rapport.

Advantages

The structure of the continuing education unit on the academic model is compatible with its internal environment. As part of the university community of departments and programs, the organization and workings of the continuing education unit are compatible with the workings of the parent institution in general. Scheduling practices, personnel practices, methods of resource computation, general faculty and administrative prestige of participation, and administrative performance expectations all unite continuing education and other academic units in a common perspective. In this model, continuing education students are also less likely to be perceived as a peripheral audience. As a result, standards applied to continuing education students are more likely to converge with those applied to conventional units' students.

Continuing education operation on the academic model also tends to increase unit availability for, and participation in, institutionally valued activities peripheral to the core continuing education function. The more the continuing education unit is structured to be, and is viewed as, organizationally mainstream, the more likely are continuing education administrators, staff, and faculty to be absorbed into the university community's work and life. The unit will contribute its share of committee members' services and unit resources; it will give its members' time to committees, planning groups, and all the other endeavors that can cause disputes as well cement ties on a campus.

MIXED MODELS: DE FACTO AND INTENDED VERSIONS

As we indicated at the outset, we believe that most continuing education units in operation combine elements of both pure types. As we also indicated, this mixture is usually de facto, and not a result of any self-scrutiny or planning. The problem with such de facto mixed-unit entities is that, bereft of rationale and of an awareness of the pure types, the de facto mix invites structural problems compounded by the lack of a vocabulary or conceptual framework for problem diagnosis. The situation precludes chances to remedy the shortcomings of such units. The shortcomings are denied, defended, attacked, and tampered with, to the detriment of continuing education functions and administrators' tempers.

The general unit orientation for de facto mixed units is unhealthy vacillation. In the attempt to be entrepreneurial, opportunities are pursued as they present themselves—often literally, as when a client offering a "gold mine" walks in the door. (Indeed, the client may walk in the door after having been referred by another office, and may have walked into many offices before finding the CE office.) At the same time, periodic audits of classroom head counts and faculty-student ratios, as well as assessments of unit heads' satisfaction with continuing education, may precipitate a quick effort to look mainstream and meet mainstream criteria.

The criteria for success are both academic and entrepreneurial, separately and simultaneously, unmelded in any way. They depend on the individual evaluator—and there may be many evaluators. Even when revenue-tracking procedures defy entrepreneurial evaluation, vague entrepreneurial rules of thumb may be applied. Even when continuing education and off-campus programs conducted by line non-CE units are entangled with continuing education unit involvement in some phases of such activities, vague academic rules of thumb may be applied. Indeed, under such circumstances evaluation may appear all thumbs.

The disadvantages of a de facto mixed unit are obvious, its advantages are nonexistent, and the unit is likely to meander. Survival is of course quite possible. It is not uncommon for certain institutional functions to be considered mandatory in large organizations, though there may be little ability or motive to perform them effectively. A titular presence for such functions in the organization may simply serve a traditional sense of what a major institution ought to have in its repertory, without any real desire to actually perform that function according to any significant performance test (Frost et al., 1985).

The de facto hybrid continuing education unit as an expression of institutional tradition tends to become modest and passive. This role is doubtless a marginally useful one. A de facto hybrid unit is not inherently scandalous, but it does represent a missed opportunity for the institution in the continuing education domain.

As indicated, we believe that the de facto mixed structure arises mostly by institutional default, for want of a conscious articulation of pure models out of which to fashion a selective mix. We presume that in university organizations there are two common reasons for the emergence of mixed models.

First, a pure type may not be possible, given the organizational realities faced by administrators who join a system already in place. Thus, at least some individuals are in mixed types simply because their universities have fallen into de facto mix through forces at work in times past. Secondly, many units may fall into this mix because there is no strong advocacy for a planned development of either pure model. In the absence of deliberate measures, one is far more likely to produce marble cake than layer cake.

We have suggested that finding an appropriate structure for continuing education units requires that the profession begin with a clear understanding of the pure types implicit in the evolution of the field to date. This allows for an understanding of the relationship between structural forms and functional and dysfunctional aspects of continuing education organization in the context of the modern university. We have noted that while the pure types provide reference points and come close to enactment in some institutions, many other institutions are likely to exhibit de facto hybrids that are best understood in light of the way they mix elements of the pure types. We also referred to the possibility—and indeed, on many grounds, desirability—of striving for a deliberate mix of elements of the pure types. We used the term "integrated model" to refer to that possibility. The remainder of this chapter is devoted to an explication of that model.

The Integrated Model

As we indicated at the outset, the key element of the appropriateness of any structural format for continuing education units (in fact, for any subunit of a large organization) is compatibility with the "missions and priorities" of the parent institution. It is now time to look more seriously at this notion.

It is characteristic of the modern university that a consensus on missions and priorities is hard to maintain beyond the level of rhetoric and vague notions. Concepts of purpose that can enlist a majority's agreement are usually so vague as to lack operational specificity. Formulations of missions and priorities with operational specificity will generally fragment the vague rhetorical consensus. Despite the strain between this view and traditional conceptualizations of what large-scale formal organizations ought to be about, more recent theories suggest this may be increasingly common in modern organizations (Thompson, 1977; Cohen & March, 1986; Lerner, 1976a; Day & Day, 1977; Weick, 1978). Without excessive theoretical digression, suffice it to say that this trend can be largely traced to the rise of professional/technical expertise as a countervailing source of authority in our modern society's organizations, rivaling traditional formal administrative power in the setting of organizational priorities and in the defense and maintenance of the legitimacy of standard operating procedures in large organizations.

This trend toward dual foci of authority means that the general administrative hierarchy is no longer the exclusive locus of organizational policy-making in many organizations. We believe that this tendency is most extreme in universities (and hospitals). Such institutions may be characterized as multiprofessional organizations. In such institutions, instead of a single expert grouping of individuals with professional credentials and knowledge ready to dispute decisions based on administrative considerations, there now exist multiple communities of experts, within and across administrative units, exhibiting a considerable degree of self-governance within a loose organization of such units. General administration seems to provide a unifying structure and codified procedures. However, the structure is a skeletal one. It cannot be the sole focus of agenda formation because substantive expert knowledge in the multiplicity of professional fields resides in the various professionalized departments. Significant substantive agendas must be negotiated (Day & Day, 1977), often with intense politicking in the context of a collegial-informal setting (Lerner, 1976a; 1976b), with considerable dramaturgy (Thompson, 1977), often with highly problematic outcomes (Cohen & March, 1986), and with the inclusion of a considerable stochastic, or probabilistic, element.

Thus, the contemporary continuing education unit, in the modern university as a multiprofessional organization, must by configured to interface with a general administrative hierarchy, but not the hierarchy alone. It must also be configured to interface with a multiplicity of research items, committees of scholars, programs, departments, institutes, centers, schools, and colleges in which reside substantive expertise and linkages to equally articulated professional communities in the external environment. Presumably the latter share with their university counterparts the substantive expertise and professional credibility to articulate a demand for continuing education. The general university hierarchy provides legitimized conflict resolution, a common denominator of procedural formality, and a broad context of internal values—the organizational culture, as it were. These processes are vital to maintaining a necessary organizational integration at the macro, systemic level (Lerner, 1976a). To be sure, considerable latitude and individual unit variation persist in the interpretation and operationalization of these general organizational themes (Lerner & Wanat, 1983). However, the continuing education unit, as a boundary actor representing the organization, must undertake to deal directly with the multitude of professionalized circles of actors within the organization as well. It is in the nature of the multiprofessional organization that general administration cannot play these roles in the aggregation and articulation of significant missions and priorities being developed throughout the institution.

With this overview of the dynamics of a university as a large and complex multiprofessional organization serving as the context of continuing education units, we are now in a position to describe the deliberate mix of entrepreneurial and academic pure types as embodied in the integrated model. The everincreasing impact of the multiprofessional ambiance of modern universities explains the apparent prevalence of de facto mixed types while underlining the importance of undertaking the deliberately integrated model.

The Features of the Integrated Model

General unit orientation. The integrated model combines an interest in entrepreneurial success with a concern for academic rigor and innovativeness. The criterion for success is profitability in offering programs confined to those which the faculty and the allied professional elite outside the university view as enhancing the state of applied professional arts in their field.

The emphasis is thus on the profitability of prestigious, innovative programs, innovation being defined jointly by the practitioner community and the scholarly community. A related goal is to enhance (or to maintain and reinforce) the reputation of the university in the eyes of the relevant professional elites. An institution supporting this model characteristically accepts that in a multiprofessional institution, the university's reputation exists in each of the independent cultures of the various community and national professional elites as well as in the population at large. Professional communities' assessments are not likely tied to symbolic activities of the institution as a whole. (By the latter we mean, for example; local economic development, public access to hospital services, athletics, availability of recreational facilities, etc.) Reputation among elite professional circles is measured by specialized professional criteria and is more susceptible to specific overtures providing intra-profession linkages. As a result, the continuing education unit on the integrated model is also judged by its success as a vehicle for initiating sustainable relationships with particular elite opinion-making groups. This adds a public affairs dimension to the continuing education unit on the integrated model.

General pattern of unit configuration. We indicated that the integrated continuing education unit should be positioned as a boundary actor representing the university to select external constituencies. This entails considerable cultivation of professional/disciplinary elites within the multiprofessional parent institution. As a result, the ideal structure for the integrated continuing education unit is one that allows it to easily and rapidly form and reform consortia of interested and relevant university participants for dealings with corresponding external groups to carry out a given project. Such a unit's culture and structural format are akin to what Bennis has called "the temporary organization" (1969). Task-force, project management–oriented structures are called for.

Most likely, integrated-model continuing education units will differentiate formal or de facto specialist administrative personnel serving under a director who coordinates clusters of professional groups around projects in a finite set of academic areas. This is necessary because considerable expertise is required even of general administrators in now specialized professional areas. Team management style in such efforts further implies a need for administrative firsts-among-equals for any of the relevant faculty groups on each project. They would be needed to provide the specialist-generalist team leadership such projects require. The logic of the model also implies similar coordinating vehicles. Advisory councils of practitioners, both project-focused and in committees of the whole, are also consistent with this model.

The CE unit on the integrated model is project-driven, team oriented, and bicultural regarding internal and external environments. It is multicultural regarding the cultures within the multiprofessional environment. Its tone is entrepreneurially aggressive, minimally procedural, and intellectually driven. Under ideal circumstances, it is perceived by external elites as the "intellectual salon" or "front parlor" of the university.

Criteria for success. The criteria for success include profit for programs justified by their representativeness of modern professional concerns to participating professional groups. A smaller profit may be acceptable if the program produces positive visibility for the institution in the eyes of the practitioner client groups affiliated with the units' programs. The indirect benefits of stimulation of faculty research interest in applied areas and the fostering of practitioner-scholar networks leading to research support may also be used as benchmarks of unit performance.

Disadvantages Units of this type run at a relatively frenetic pace and their members are likely to experience their work in terms of extreme "highs" and "lows." This is because the units are project-driven and are also intensely collegial, informal, and interactive in internal style.

Roles overlap and duplicate one another; working teams shift memberships through frequent reconfiguration for new tasks. Intra-organizational diplomacy is vital, both within the unit and in dealings with faculty groups, who now share in project development. These subtleties are complicated by yet a third group of actors—external elite groups who may be either clients or links to clients. The result can be a high level of organizational and individual operating stress. Greater substantive intellectual breadth is also expected of the unit director and staff.

Advantages Many of the advantages of the integrated model are among the features we listed as disadvantages above, now viewed in a different light. For example, a unit style that is intensely collegial, informal, and interactive may be congenial to some participants. Ideally, persons recruited for such units will be those who gravitate to such environments. Likewise, while duplication and overlap cannot produce an administratively streamlined profile, duplication and overlap as a "functional redundancy" have been viewed as an asset in some organization theory circles concerned with organizational design (Lerner, 1986; Bendor, 1985; Landau, 1969). They allow great flexibility in the event of unforeseen difficulties that might cripple more rigid structures. Such units not only change with the times more easily, they are often creators of the changes.

Similarly, the increased skill in organizational diplomacy and increased political sensitivity required in the integrated model may be viewed as merely the sign of such a unit's being ideally situated as a meeting point of interests. The unit may be seen as providing a natural vehicle for spanning the psychological distance between disciplinary units that have more in common than their members might at first realize.

Also, when well developed, this diplomatic function can bring outside groups together with "academics," serving to further break down adverse stereotyping. It is a service not only to the university but to society as well if elite circles outside the university understand that "academic" does not mean irrelevant, and if academics understand that scholars are not the only intellectuals.

The final consequence of operating continuing education units on the integrated model is again one that may be viewed perhaps negatively as well as positively. However, in choosing to end on an optimistic note, we explore it under the heading of advantages while noting its problems.

It is clear that the continuing education unit on the integrated model is well configured to project the image of the parent institution to the outside world, the external organizational environment. This implies that the overarching mission of the integrated continuing education unit must be as clear to the leadership of the parent institution as it is within the unit, or to external clients.

The openness of the integrated unit model, the permeability of its structure, makes it impossible to sustain a sense of mission apart from the parent institution's vision. If the leadership of the parent institution is confused and inconsistent in this regard, the integrated continuing education unit is not insular enough to escape this confusion. Such is the potential disadvantage of this structural situation.

More optimistically, if the leadership of the parent institution offers a consistent sense of purpose and mission stemming from a clear institutional sense of self, then the integrated unit model becomes a leading unit in the presentation of institutional self, projecting the desired image outward. The image it thereby presents also educates internal audiences in this regard, better acculturating them to the organization, as they observe what the organization means to be by how it presents itself externally. A further implication of these circumstances is that the leadership of continuing education units on the integrated model must become part of the strategic planning work group of the parent institution. Only then can the continuing education unit focus on the strategically primary elements of the institutional self-image intended for projection to the external environment. Without the involvement of the continuing education unit in the strategic planning process of the parent institution, the images projected by the institution will be blurred for lack of intra-organizational coordination.

SUMMARY

This chapter has endeavored to show that pure types exist upon which to fashion continuing education unit structures. Each involves attendant alterations in general unit orientation, structural configuration, criteria of success applied, and inherent advantages and disadvantages in operation. Moreover, the frequency of mixed models, far from diluting the value of understanding pure types, indicates the necessity of understanding pure types as a prerequisite to making sense of the empirically observable hybrids. The failure to attain a conceptual grasp of the issues in the pure models invites hybrids de facto, by institutional default.

The consequences in such circumstances is the risk of the worst of both worlds in a mixture of conflicting expectations. The preferred and feasible alternative form of mixed model, our "integrated model," is attainable with a proper appreciation of the pure elements to be combined in it. To this must be added an appreciation of the multiprofessional context of the modern university and of the pressures and opportunities it brings. We have outlined structural features and internal dynamics of a purposefully integrated mixed model. They were developed through an appreciation of the interplay between the needs of the multiprofessional institution and the dynamics of the pure continuing education models.

We have in no way intended to belittle the pure models. They can work for those who have made the corresponding value choices. However, we hope that the healthy continuous discussion of structural formats for continuing education delivery by continuing education units may now focus more profitably on the issues raised by the integrated model for the multiprofessional context. A dialogue devoted to the further exploration of this context would seem to promise fresh insights and new knowledge, which could in turn be applied to revitalize our common agenda.

REFERENCES

Bendor, J. (1985). *Parallel systems: Redundancy in government*. Berkeley: University of California Press.

Bennis, W. G. (1969, July–August). Post-bureaucratic leadership, *Transaction*, p. 45.

Cohen, M., & March, J. (1986). *Leadership and ambiguity: The American college president*. Boston: Harvard Business School Press.

Day, R. & Day, J. (1977, Winter). A review of the current state of negotiated order theory: An appreciation and critique. *Sociological Quarterly, 18*(1).

Frost, P. J., et al. (1985). *Organizational culture*. Beverly Hills: Sage Publications.

Katz, D., & Kahn, R. L. (1978). *The social psychology of organizations* (2nd ed.). New York: Wiley.

Landau, M. (1969). Redundancy, rationality, and the problems of duplication and overlap. *Public Administration Review, 39*, 346–358.

Lerner, A. (1976a). *The politics of decision making.* Beverly Hills: Sage Publications.

Lerner, A. (1976b). *Experts, politicians, and decision making in the technological society.* Morristown, NJ: General Learning Press.

Lerner, A. (1986, February). Ambiguity and organizational analysis: The consequences of micro versus macro conceptualization. *Administration & Society, 17*(4), 461–479.

Lerner, A. (1986, November). There is more than one way to be redundant. *Administration & Society, 18*(3), 334–359.

Lerner, A., & Wanat, J. (1983, November–December). Fuzziness and bureaucracy. *Public Administration Review, 43*(6), 500–510.

Taylor, W. (1978). Scientific management. In J. Shafritz & A. Hyde (Eds.), *Classics of public administration.* Oak Park, Illinois: Moore Publishing Co.

Thompson, V. (1977). *Modern organization* (2nd ed.). University, AL: University of Alabama Press.

Weick, K. (1976, December). Educational organizations as loosely coupled systems. *Administrative Science Quarterly, 23*, 541–552.

Weick, K. (1979). *The social psychology of organizing* (2nd ed.). Reading, MA: Addison Wesley.

Wilensky, H. (1967). *Organizational intelligence.* New York: Basic Books.

6   *A Question of Finance: Existing Resources and New Missions*

B. Kay King

The financial context of the coming wave is expected to be characterized by a continual decline in traditional resource allocations occurring simultaneously with increasing external demands for educational access by a variety of influential publics. Although these pressures will especially affect public universities, private institutions will also feel them. Chancellors, presidents, and provosts will be required to make financial choices heretofore unnecessary. The choices will range from program cuts and retrenchment, based on traditional resource mechanisms, to the creation of viable financial strategies that will allow the institution to maintain all core missions and priorities under increasing and often conflicting pressures.

The decade of the 1980s saw a jumble of financial management strategies, with most research institutions opting to reduce financial support for those activities and services perceived as peripheral to the "pure" research mission. Dollars were pooled and used to retain premier research faculty. Resources for service offices, including those for administrative staff, secretarial staff, and even graduate assistants, were reduced. As a result, decisions regarding strategies for efficient institutional responses to impending social and political demands were postponed.

The public service mission, which has lost institutional prestige during the past three or four decades, especially at research universities, is expected to gain stature as external demands require a "looking outward" for survival. Reduced resources and higher demands will force university leadership to create financial alternatives to retrenchment. Accompanying the increased value ascribed to the public service function is the need to create policies and systems that will bring the public service function into the mainstream of university prestige. It is predicted that the continuing education (CE) organization, as an arm of the public service mission, and with its history of functioning as an entrepreneurial island within the ocean of institutional tradition and bureaucratic financial systems, can provide the parent institution with viable financial strategies for addressing these external demands.

A premise of this chapter is that universities will be required to become more businesslike in their financial practices if they are to survive an economic decline. Specifically, universities may be forced to shift their prevailing strategy of funding from one of subsidy to one of self-support. Matkin (1985) addresses the financial implications for continuing education units as subsidies are reduced;

> In subsidized organizations, this [reduction of subsidies] can be viewed as a movement toward self-support, whereas self-supporting parent institution requirements for greater financial returns from the CE organization can be viewed as a movement toward the for-profit model of business enterprise. (p. 3)

Rather than viewing the parent institution's financial situation as influencing the CE organization, however, this chapter suggests that the continuing education unit can influence the finances of the organization. It can achieve this by providing the parent institution with proven and tested financial planning systems and strategies that have enabled continuing education to function as a cost-recovery business. Therefore, a second premise of this chapter is that the continuing education function can provide policies and associated mechanisms by which universities can address financial issues during an era of declining resources. To achieve this, however, institutions must recognize the unique capabilities of continuing education as a means for responding to external constituencies.

Visionary university leaders, who recognize the connection between new demands and the response structures already in place in continuing education, can play a vital role in securing financial survival. Continuing education directors, who have for the past two decades dealt with the issue of their units' marginality, must help university leadership to recognize continuing education as a valuable problem-solving resource available to them (Votruba, 1987; Winters, 1991). They must alert leadership to the flexibility of systems, mechanisms, and policies that have been developed to ensure responsiveness and enhance image.

This chapter focuses on the strategic thinking that will be required of university leaders as they develop and integrate new financial planning strategies. The first section focuses on the historical relationships among the outreach (public service) mission, prestige, and finance. The second section elaborates on this theme by focusing on several institutional behaviors and characteristics that have curtailed the development of cost-recovery planning strategies. These behaviors, well known to continuing education units, have inhibited the responsiveness of the institution to external demands for programming.

The third section suggests a conceptual framework for financial planning amid the decline of traditional appropriations and subsidies. Finally, the fourth section gives examples of response mechanisms that can help universities cope with dwindling traditional financial sources. Examples of active collaborations, which allow various entities of the university community to form and re-form for the purpose of addressing the educational needs of external clients, are presented as a major strategy for managing financial decline. Through these alliances, universities can showcase their strengths, rather than trying to emulate other providers and thereby duplicating programming and services. The contractual agreement that defines specific collaborations between the institution and external constituencies for the provision of university-sponsored instruction, as developed by continuing education units, is the symbol of this change. These types of financial arrangements are expected to share institutional prestige and credibility with contracts or grants for sponsored research.

Since the 1930s, sponsored research has served universities as the major indicator of productivity and image. The generation of external dollars by faculty and departments for the support of research is viewed as a major factor in assessing institutional prestige and faculty worth. However, while this was occurring, continuing education directors, often working with faculty, developed contractual agreements with a variety of external constituencies, including corporations, agencies, and school districts. These arrangements generated dollars, enhanced image, responded to external demands, and fulfilled a central educational role, yet were never valued by university elite on a par with those dollars generated by sponsored research efforts. The final section of this chapter addresses the type of thinking that continuing education directors must embrace in order to enhance credibility for the entrepreneurially innovative, yet institutionally acceptable financial planning strategies characteristic of continuing education. This decade will require of continuing education leadership a mind-set that transcends old issues of marginality and institutional acceptability. The tide of the future is innovation and its flow is through continuing education.

OUTREACH: THE THIRD MISSION

Responding to the educational needs and social problems of a broad cadre of external publics has been a fundamental, unique aspect of American public universities since their establishment under the Morrill Act over a century ago (DiBiaggio, 1987). Although the Morrill Act embodies noble principles, the degree to which state legislatures and other external funding agencies have supported their application has varied, contingent upon such factors as public pressure and cash flow. Furthermore, the extent to which university leadership has used state allocations for its outreach mission has varied in proportion to the prestige connected with external endeavors.

Historically, the amount of funding committed to public universities by state and federal legislatures has been directly related to the broader economic conditions and policy priorities of a particular era (Dahl, 1980; Knowles, 1970). The demand for university education has generally outdistanced the availability of resources to pay for its provision, but rarely to the extent seen in the past decade and likely to be seen in the near future.

With many public universities suffering financial shortages, continuing education organizations are widely and routinely expected to become sources for generating new funds to support traditional university agendas. At the same time, and partly in order to spur such entrepreneurship, continuing education administrators are frequently forced to compete with academic deans for the same, often dwindling, internal resources. This competition can create conflict between the school's traditional and the nontraditional missions, represented by academic deans and continuing education administrators respectively.

Deal (1987) comments on this conflict:

> Tension between traditional and non-traditional programs in colleges and universities has always existed. However, recent demographic shifts may intensify these tensions into deeper conflicts. . . . Resources generated by continuing education are frequently used to subsidize traditional programs, even though regular faculty typically look with disdain upon their non-traditional colleagues. (p. 89)

While the traditional culture of the academy resists notions of internal financial competition and income generation, defining a role in the marketplace has often been a major function of the continuing education organization. This emphasis on market niche is necessitated by the expectation that CE units will be financially solvent to one degree or another (King & Lerner, 1987). Continuing education administrators are no strangers to bottom-line expectations.

In the latter half of the 1980s, universities were faced with a declining traditional-age student population, and with pressures from state legislative bodies for accountability through zero-based budgeting. Universities were expected to respond with financial systems focused on earnings, rather than relying on an unending supply of resources appropriated through annual allocation processes. Belt-tightening occurred especially in those categories perceived as peripheral to core institutional functioning — for example, administrative support services, student support services, financial aid, and physical plant repairs. In practice, cost containment in the late 1980s had a minimal impact on the hiring of core faculty or on other budget practices that supported the primary research mission. In the very near future, however, even the most sheltered of professors are likely to experience first-hand the impacts of those external forces affecting the organization. Salaries may remain stable or decline, competition for flexible funds for experimental programming and research will increase even more, and accountability will be reflected in productivity measures unfamiliar to academics. They will be introduced to the business context with which their continuing education units have long been familiar.

Under such a scenario, continuing education units are likely to be recognized as profit centers for their parent institutions. A positive result of this development will be a new institutional credibility for continuing education units, albeit on financial grounds at least as much as on pedagogic grounds. Establishment of a common language between university and external players should lead to the types of joint intellectual partnerships that have been so difficult to develop in the past. Continuing education units are well positioned to anchor much of the university's participation in such relationships, especially in the early stages.

The demographic, social, and economic changes occurring in the university's external environment may require corresponding changes in the traditional bureaucratic structures of higher education, including their financial operation. Elaborate systems of administrative approval, which were commonplace in times of financial stability at the institutional level, are likely to break down when external changes require a streamlining of response systems. Instead, several individual and organizational patterns of response are likely to characterize the continuing education units' repositioning in the confusion of this changing environment.

By creating financial planning models and their associated systems and methodologies, continuing education may provide a mechanism for maintaining institutional wellness in the upcoming era. Financial procedures ideally suited to these new demands include a variety of individual and collaborative formats for contracting with external constituencies. Internal, formalized partnerships, transcending traditional appropriations structures, are also likely to be favored for their ability to streamline institutional finances and limit unproductive duplication of services.

Such formalized partnerships involve joint planning between units within the university community and external organizations, particularly regarding risk capital, profit-sharing, direct and indirect cost budgeting, and fees and tuition assessments. These distinctive arrangements are well suited to the projected financial future because they allow maximum administrative efficiency without threatening the core policies and values of the institution.

When such limited partnerships between the university and a specific external agency, industry, or corporation are viewed as financially advantageous arrangements and are focused on specific program ventures, the perennial issues of institutional mission and academic prerogatives need not encumber the delivery of continuing education programs. Institutional values can be protected by clear statements of ground rules for such partnerships. Also, when the parties take care to affirm the prerogatives left outside the partnership, then principles of mission and academic autonomy may in fact be more clearly stated than they would otherwise be. Having made this general observation, we will reserve our future discussion of institutional and scholarly values in relationship to financial planning for a later section of this chapter.

INSTITUTIONAL BEHAVIORS: CHARACTERISTICS AND PATTERNS

A premise of this chapter is that upcoming economic circumstances will create within institutions of higher education a climate of financial awareness heretofore unknown to academic administrators. Financial practices that reward indiscriminate spending will no longer be acceptable. An example of such spending is the unplanned, seemingly frantic spending by individual departments or colleges of unused appropriation dollars at the end of the fiscal year, sometimes on unneeded equipment and services. The "if you don't spend the dollars, you'll lose the dollars" mind-set cannot be tolerated if the institution is to survive in leaner times.

New financial incentive systems will need to be developed that reward individual units for practicing financial management strategies benefiting the broader institution. As Strand (1990) has noted,

> Today competing demands force state colleges and universities to make hard choices about the amount of resources that should be allocated to teaching, research, and public service. Forces within as well as outside the campus compete vigorously for the time, energy, and funding to promote their particular interests. Unless the institution and its leadership have established a definite plan for subdividing resources among teaching research and public service, administrators are often perplexed when making resource allocation decisions and criticized for those decisions after they are made. (p. 101)

To establish the framework under which financial planning models will evolve, it may be helpful to first analyze several practices typically engaged in by universities that can hinder productive financial planning practices. Four such behaviors are dominance, parochialism, transference, and delay.

Dominance

Dominance refers to activities by the parent institution aimed at controlling revenue for traditional hierarchical units through traditional allocation processes. Dominance is rationalized by varying interpretations of institutional mission through ritualized recitations, which are often made obsolete by a rapidly changing economic environment. Dominance can be perpetuated in a hierarchical environment in which leadership may establish elaborate processes for control under a variety of planning rubrics. This behavioral orientation represents the triumph of bureaucratic dramaturgy over sound financial practice and true institutional mission.

Departmental dominance places faculty members who actively participate in continuing education activities in an especially vulnerable position. Traditionally, their primary source of financial reward has been the academic unit. Under the dominance mind-set, faculty members are placed under the emotional strain of meeting the requirements of their home departments so as to merit the financial rewards associated with academic success, while attempting, at the same time, to fulfill the educational needs of nontraditional learners.

A commonsense solution to this dilemma is to redistribute appropriations to support both priorities. Lynton and Elman's (1987) "second-stream" approach provides for redistribution of existing resources according to a model that affirms the role of continuing education programming. This shifting of the dominant distribution mode is a step toward the type of thinking that will be needed for the future. However, a further expansion of models of this type, which lessen the competition between the traditional and nontraditional for limited appropriated resources, will be critical to institutional growth in the approaching era.

Parochialism

Parochialism consists of a series of behaviors whereby unit interests are raised above all others. More than any other factor within the institution, dwindling resources contribute to the parochial preoccupation with unit interests. Sufferers from parochialism perceive that they are in direct competition with both peers and the parent institution for a fixed number of dollars. In the most common scenario, academic units scramble for individual survival under what they consider a fixed resource ceiling. Within the formal, administrative hierarchy of the university, administrative retrenchment by college-level administrators may obscure a vision of the parent organization's overall financial needs. In such circumstances, such a penny-wise/pound foolish outlook, born of short-term preoccupation with costs may inhibit the type of strategic planning necessary for institutional solvency.

In such a climate, the immediate response of unit administrators faced with the order to contain costs may be to eliminate "peripheral" areas in order to protect the core. Consequent budget reductions at universities often translate into a disproportionate elimination of vital support services — in many cases, the very services that maintain core functions. These expenditure categories include graduate assistantships, secretarial positions, travel funds, and facilities maintenance. In extreme cases, such a retrenchment mentality, which focuses less on making money than on saving money, may induce the thinning of the junior faculty ranks so essential to the long-range health of institutions. Such measures taken against line units can set off a process that further fuels polarization among units, inhibits entrepreneurship, and obscures institutional interests and the need for financial planning to support such interests.

Transference

The transference of costs from one unit to another, under the misconception that total costs are thereby being contained, is another form of limited financial vision. In actuality, the parent organization must still absorb the initial cost, and may, in fact, experience an increase in its burden if the unit receiving the cost is unprepared to comply with the added expense, or is unable to meet the expense as efficiently as a unit practiced in dealing with it.

When the university suffers from this transference syndrome, continuing education units often find themselves in the position of appearing to compete with departments for funding. Because continuing education units are often under a mandate for cost recovery, they usually must charge a fee for services rendered to a particular project. One such illustration describes this behavior.

Continuing education professionals of a centralized office are finalizing the program budget with a department head. The department head, thinking to save money, suggests that they eliminate line items designed to support continuing education staff. These costs include fees for its graphics artists and registration specialists. Concurrently, the head decides to assign these functions to the departmental secretary.

On the surface, the budget appears to be streamlined through this process, and yet, in actuality, the parent institution has merely experienced a transferred financial burden. The departmental secretary has been assigned extra duties, which are likely to take time from the work for which the secretary was hired. Furthermore, the departmental secretary probably will not be as effective in performing the new programming responsibilities as would the continuing education staff, skilled in these specific areas. Also, by cutting the continuing education revenue from the budget, the department head has influenced the overall, long-range solvency of the continuing education unit functioning under a mandate of cost recovery. Either the continuing education unit or the parent institution must absorb this cost, or ultimately continuing education staff must be reduced. Most continuing education units can survive one such decision. However, if the transference syndrome spreads, then eventually qualified staff will be eliminated due to a loss of their source of support.

Circumstances that allow individual academic departments to make unilateral financial decisions cannot be tolerated in the future. Placing power over such decisions at the lowest unit level wreaks havoc on the consistent, long-range service capability of the parent institution, especially its ability to maintain a professional continuing education function.

As a centralized academic support unit, continuing education provides a wide variety of administrative services for programs, from marketing through registration. These services are paid for with fee revenue or through the recovery of indirect costs. Therefore, accurate cost recovery planning by continuing education directors requires an acceptable degree of assurance that the fees generated will support continuing education staff and administration. When the transference syndrome is tolerated, it is virtually impossible to plan for consistent fee revenue generation. Furthermore, due to the inconsistency of the transference behavior, the institution may project an image of disorganization to those constituencies who expect consistent, responsive service.

If university-wide budget reductions are made from a narrow perspective, without a careful analysis of their impact across line units, they can have a domino effect. Expenditures are not reduced, but merely reorganized into unfamiliar divisions of labor. In an attempt to continue vital functions, individual units must now (less efficiently) pick up functions that centralized units formerly performed. Centralized units providing organization-wide support functions now decentralize and transfer such functions to less proficient units. The latter perform less efficiently what centralized units performed better and less redundantly. More likely than not the reduction of critical centralized support services will not contribute to the total cost containment of the institution, but rather will create additional costs as efforts are duplicated and units forced to learn new functions spend more time at the things they do worst.

Delay

More than any other practice, delay in responding to the demands of clientele has the potential to inhibit the external generation of funding through continuing education. Traditionally, "timeliness" holds a different meaning for the bureaucratic university than it does for private industry, whose survival is contingent upon a sensitivity to changing markets. Large, complex universities place great value on elongated review processes. These may, due to their inherent delay features, contribute to the frustration level of external partners accustomed to efficient response. This is not to imply that procedures embodying essential values of the institution, such as academic review processes that ensure faculty and program integrity, should be eliminated. However, when universities allow delay to characterize their business practices and are unable to distinguish between academic and business subcultures, they may lose their credibility with external providers. The streamlining of business response systems will be an essential characteristic in the future.

The following section focuses on strategies that will be needed for effective financial planning of continuing education and related unit activities. We will raise several issues which will have to be addressed by university administrators within and without the ranks of continuing education, if they are to ride the coming wave and not be drowned by it.

FINANCIAL PLANNING: STRATEGIES AND MECHANISMS

This section focuses on strategies that would seem to best ensure effective financial negotiating postures by continuing education administrators as new requirements surface. Continuing education professionals tend to be relatively sophisticated in their knowledge of budgeting, perhaps because continuing education's history of emphasizing cost recovery has required the development of such skills. Calculating direct and indirect costs and demonstrating the ability to generate profits are practical requirements of virtually all continuing education units. Given this assumption, the following discussion focuses on analytical issues and the organizational context for continuing education, rather than describing the "how-to" of budget development. Those interested in the latter are referred to *Effective Budgeting in Continuing Education* (Matkin, 1985).

Dynamic Contractual Collaborations

In the future universities will be asked by new and diverse external constituencies to play an ever more active role in solving a wide variety of social and educational problems. Some of these problems may be appropriately addressed under existing parameters for public service and will compliment the institution's existing research and teaching missions. However, other problems, such as literacy and wellness, which reflect demographic and economic dynamics, more than likely will force universities to evaluate their traditional response mechanisms and either to adjust to these new demands in institutionally viable ways or to retrench and withdraw from the changes. For universities that opt for change, a proposed financial planning strategy is the formation of numerous "dynamic contractual collaborations" between and among university entities and external constituencies.

Although the concept of collaboration is not new to universities, in practice, traditional financial collaborations have tended to carry elements of domination by one institution and/or competition among many. Virtually every state has created some form of educational regulatory body to deter competition and control duplication of programming. Consortia of one form or another appear and disappear, yet competition continues. Under future dynamics, however, it is suggested that competition and domination can be tempered by the creation of dynamic contractual collaborations. These collaborations are financial planning strategies in which the university and an external party or parties enter into a written contractual agreement that matches educational and service needs with explicit capabilities of the providers.

The "dynamic" component requires that the contractual collaborations reflect an analysis of external forces affecting the collaborations, such as economic limitations and demographic shifts. In contrast, collaborations characteristically defined as "static" are those in which one member, usually the provider of the instruction, presents a fixed program of study, which is accepted "as is" by the second partner in the collaboration. This static relationship, common in contractual arrangements prior to the new era, represents the "canned" program syndrome.

In the dynamic collaboration, it is assumed that each player comes to the collaboration with a set of financial wares, both assets and liabilities, which must be factored into the planning process. Their consideration is an element of the collaboration. In addition, each partner brings to the process a set of external pressures that affect its ability to plan. The need to disclose, analyze, and adjust to these forces becomes an element in the dynamic planning process.

To veteran continuing education administrators accustomed to managing cost-effective collaborations, this may raise a question regarding the distinction between new strategies for financial planning and those they have been practicing for decades. After all, mature consultation is not necessarily a monopoly of the future. However, the distinguishing factor is the extent to which this thinking will be adopted by the parent institution, in its response to new demands.

In the past, adequate funding and a satisfactory (in conventional terms) caliber of undergraduate and graduate students afforded universities the luxury of a lethargic attitude toward external demands. In the future, however, such complacency has the potential to erode the institution's basic missions. Lynton and Elman (1987) suggest that academia has not shifted from its research emphasis since the 1930s. If this is indeed the case, then the changes of the coming wave have the potential for creating a maelstrom, or at the very least a minor hurricane, within the academic sea.

New for continuing education directors, who have created flexible client-focused financial mechanisms, is the degree to which they will be recognized for their abilities to guide and facilitate processes for effective collaborations. The distinguishing factor of future dynamic collaborations will be the need for the parent institution to adopt contracts for educational programming and services that allow for open, willing assessments by the parties regarding explicit capabilities and needs. Quality of education and conventionality of format must be uncoupled.

This flexibility comes none too soon. Economic turbulence will significantly affect the level of traditional funding appropriations and endowments received by institutions. Institutions clinging to admission, recruitment, and support service practices that functioned effectively in earlier times will suffer the most. Those that adapt, creating flexible and relevant educational opportunities, are expected to survive the economic shifts (Levine & Associates, 1990).

Concurrently, external publics from industry, labor, government, and the general citizenry will expect institutions of higher education to help solve complex social problems. Support from these publics will be contingent upon successfully meeting expectations. Accountability in teaching, in the provision of service, and in access will not only be desired by those seeking higher education, but will be demanded by publics expecting results in return for resources provided. "The new university is an institution less clearly defined than the traditional one; it is more closely interrelated with its surroundings, and it is in fact a part of the context in which it operates" (Lynton & Elman, 1987, p. 162).

This advocacy for creating flexible support services and budgeting mechanisms cannot be perceived as an advocacy for lessening academic standards, which would destroy the foundation of the academy. Advocating change in the complex procedures required for admission, for example, should not be seen as advocating the lowering of admission standards. Advocating student intervention and retention strategies should not be perceived as advocating decreased quality of instruction. Similarly, creating a financial reward system that compensates those faculty who develop unique instructional strategies in response to future demands should not be allowed to contaminate the promotion and tenure process.

Rather, those institutions embracing the changes will need to distinguish actual institutional values from convoluted, yet often sacred, bureaucratic practices that have somehow survived in the name of academic integrity. The evaluation of the workaday academic culture must be an ongoing process (Edelson, 1990).

Although flexibility in procedures and systems is advocated as a vital element of the management of finance under new demands, this flexibility should not be interpreted as a license to violate or abuse the core financial policies of the institution. Flexible financial planning strategies as administered through continuing education must adhere to all legal practices of the institution. Entrepreneurship can and must be tied to sound financial practices. An entrepreneurial outlook can nurture compliance with such standards, arguably more readily than does the laxity of the business-as-usual approach. The intervening variable is leadership that grasps the issues and the techniques they require (Bennis & Nanus, 1985).

Components of the Contract Document

Although contractual mechanisms have been used by continuing education for over a decade, their adoption by the parent institution as a vehicle for the transfer of knowledge may be the single best means for establishing cost-effective, program-centered relationships. A key element in this technique, however, is that each partner in the collaboration both contributes to and benefits from the process. The language of the contract, rather than clouding this goal, should establish parameters, actions, and understandings.

Contractual mechanisms are favored by continuing education because they are an explicit method for defining the costs of delivering a program of study or service. In addition, when conditions of the contract are mutually agreed to by collaborating parties, it is more likely that the results of the contract will satisfy all those involved. Issues of academic rigor, applicability, and relevance can be addressed prior to contractual closure. Continuing education is uniquely positioned to achieve both its program delivery mission and its financial mandate through this mechanism. Contracts also minimize the need to cancel courses based of insufficient revenue, a common problem with the open enrollment courses prevalent in continuing education programs. Contracts provide a mechanism for reducing up-front risk capital while guaranteeing a fixed amount of revenue sufficient to accomplish the agreed activity. Critical to the success of the continuing education contract is attention to core components of the written agreement. The following elements are basic to any contractual collaboration. (Of course, the elaboration of each component is contingent upon the complexity of the variables.)

Actors. The contract should describe the actors who will participate in the collaboration, the powers and limitations of each, and the auspices under which each is operating. Typically, contractual agreements include a description both of those providing the service or program and of those receiving it. Individual actors should carry the authority to make decisions on behalf of their organizations, or should have immediate access to decision-making channels.

Type of program or service to be provided. A complete description of the instructional program and/or service(s) to be provided under the auspices of the contract is a component critical to the satisfaction of all parties involved. Characteristic of the new thinking, external actors in the contract will expect programs to provide specific outcomes immediately beneficial to the organizations the external actors represent. Universities, traditionally sensitive to external interventions in curricular decision-making, may find demands for practical applications of knowledge discomforting. Therefore, program definition and a shared understanding of educational expectations are essential. The success of these discussions will be contingent upon the negotiating and clarifying capabilities of the continuing education actors, who should possess the expertise to understand the motives and cultures of all parties.

The category of course or program is defined in language comprehensible to each actor in the collaboration. The credit course and conference are program categories familiar to academia. However, even under these rubrics, deferential perceptions of delivery strategies and requirements exist. For example, from the external actor's perspective, holding classes on the corporate premises may contribute to optimal use of employee time. On the other hand, from the university actor's perspective, this location may not provide adequate access to reference materials. Such issues, although seemingly minor, often require diplomacy and negotiation. The recognized expertise of the continuing education professional in these areas may be expanded as new constituencies require new elements of accountability in contractual agreements.

In previous eras, contractual negotiations were often blocked when the university actor declared that academic freedom was being threatened or when the external actor claimed that academia was not sensitive to industrial needs for practical applications. At this point CE professionals played a vital role as negotiators, sensitive to the conflict between theory and practice, understanding the need for a learning-centered approach, yet cognizant of the institutional values they represented. The changing demands and expectations of those constituencies who support universities will require creative solutions that protect institutional integrity yet overcome the obstacles of past decades.

Students/participants.   Those individuals or categories of individuals who will participate in the program of instruction should be defined in the context of their readiness to learn. This context may include an evaluation of their potential to successfully complete the defined program of study, expressed according to traditional university admission criteria as well as more nontraditional predictors of success for adult learners, such as experience, technical expertise, and general knowledge.

One must be aware, however, that not all potential students will meet the criteria of either category. The new learner may be deficient in a variety of areas. What role, if any, the university, especially the comprehensive research university, will play educating or reeducating the underprepared constituencies of the next decade will be a major policy issue in the future. Perhaps continuing education, through its ability to develop multiple collaborations among various categories of educational providers, will provide a mechanism for response that protects institutional integrity under the coming wave demands.

Integrated services.   The success of adult learners in traditional academia has often been directly related to the level of support services provided (Cross, 1981). Systems for streamlined and accessible registration, counseling, and numerous other support services designed by continuing education to promote the recruitment and retention of adult learners will be essential to the educational development of new constituencies. Accessible library and computer facilities, tutors, hot lines to faculty, videotapes of lectures, peer group discussions, and supplemental lessons on critical thinking are only a few of the tested services of continuing education that can be incorporated into contracts to enhance the potential success of new constituencies of learners.

Resource analysis.   The specific element of the contract often defined first is the amount of dollars that are needed to implement the program of study or services. The success of any contract is contingent upon the careful structuring of dollars under a mutually agreed-on formula bene-fiting all parties. This strategy requires a careful analysis of the assets each actor brings to the negotiation and an associated cost for that component. Bottom-line thinking may be more familiar to the profit-oriented actors of potential contractual agreements than to the not-for-profit actors, who may be accustomed to variable and often mysterious formulas for indirect cost distribution. Academia, entrenched in a history of appropriations financing and "hold-onto-everything-you-have" reward systems, may need the assis-tance of the continuing education professional to assess the fair value of services and expertise.

Furthermore, the continuing educator must understand and respect the fact that traditional academicians may come to the negotiations with, at the least, embarrassment about the very process of financial negotiation. At the worst, they disdain the "dirty business" of financial discussions. Therefore, the continuing educator should confer with the faculty member or administrator before any collective meeting of the parties involved, in order to clarify the parameters and ward off potential embarrassment.

Similarly, each party must enter into the negotiation with an under-standing that mutually agreed-on contributions will be reflected in mutually agreed-on remuneration. In academia, hidden costs, especially those of support offices such as the records office or even, in some instances, the continuing education office, are often perceived by academic units as do-nated services paid for by some unknown generous provider. As resources decline, astute leadership should recognize that these hidden costs are in fact real and impact directly on both the unit and organizational levels (Matkin, 1985).

Regardless of whether the hidden cost is directly attributable to the continuing education office or to another entity of the campus, it must be factored into the total cost formula.

When considering potential hidden costs, the continuing education professional should recognize all entities of the parent institution that will be responsible for supporting the success of the contract. This is important, because those units providing service should be reimbursed directly. This strategy should foster goodwill among units. Furthermore, one should ex-pect a higher quality and greater diversity of services than would be pro-vided if they were considered part of the normal course of university busi-ness.

Sponsoring authority. The contractual document should be reviewed and approved by key organizational offices responsible for academic and/or fiscal decision-making. These include the legal counsel, the office of business affairs, and the provost (representing academic policies), as well as the individual actors of the contract, such as the continuing education director or the dean of the sponsoring college. Likewise, the contract should be reviewed and approved by key decision-makers representing the external constituencies involved in the collaboration.

The process of internal review, although it may seem cumbersome to continuing education professionals accustomed to working with "letters of agreement" or other informal relationships, serves two major purposes. First, it adds a degree of credibility to the process of contracting for sponsored instruction, just as it does to the process of contracing for sponsored research. Second, and even more important, it brings the totality of university resources into the process.

Evaluation. Methods of evaluation are familiar components of most academic programs and are highly valued by both internal and external actors. Therefore, this component is essential for the assessment of both the process and the outcomes of the collaboration. Strategically, contractual collaborations are highly visible. Therefore, it is in the best interests of the university to insist that the evaluation of both the progress and success of contractual agreements be built into the process of implementation and not be left until the program is completed, as often occurs in traditional academia. External actors expect accountability. If the mechanisms for measuring this are not effective, then the institution may suffer a loss of credibility. Therefore, a strategy for intervening evaluation, mutually understood by all parties, and the negotiation of funding to support this activity are essential to the success of the collaboration.

COLLABORATIONS IN PRACTICE

This section presents three examples of financial planning collaborations developed through continuing education, with accompanying illustrations. Each model is analyzed by answering the following: What does the model include? To what pitfalls is it vulnerable in traditional academic contexts? How can it be refashioned to respond to new demands?

Corporate/Agency Contractual Collaboration (ccc) Model

The corporate/agency contractual collaboration (ccc) is an example of a financial model in which the university enters into a written agreement with a specific external constituency whereby it agrees to provide a recognized program of sponsored instruction to members of that group. Such constituencies include businesses and industries, hospitals, schools, governmental agencies, and associations. The full costs of offering the defined educational experience are covered by the external constituency. Full costs include all direct instructional expenses, as well as indirect support expenses.

A program of sponsored instruction is an approved format of study, defined under academic statutes, such as those of the educational policy committee of the faculty senate, the executive committee of the graduate college, or the curriculum committees of various colleges. Sponsorship implies academic review. Therefore, the continuing education professional must always be knowledgeable about and supportive of those program characteristics to which the institution lends its academic sanction. Acceptable formats include the credit course, the degree program, the noncredit workshop, and the certificate program.

A second and equally important requirement of the CCC is that the course of instruction be developed in response to specific learning needs of the defined constituency who will receive the instruction. Needs must be mutually identified and understood by all actors. It is at this juncture that the continuing education professional plays a vital role in the negotiation process. While working with the external constituency to define educational needs and relate these to specific learning outcomes, the continuing educator must always maintain the core academic values reflected in academic sponsorship. This is especially true when the format is the credit course or degree program. As Donaldson (1990) suggests,

> Because programming results in the awarding of course credit, certificates and even degrees—coins of the higher education realm second only in importance to research and publication—credit programming is a jealously guarded commodity of the higher education community. This jealousy is compounded because faculty and the institutional academic leadership are apprehensive that continuing education credit courses and programs may fail to meet quality standards. (pp. 3–4)

Vulnerability of the CCC model in the traditional academic context. Under the auspices of one or more recognized unit of the institution, such as the office of grants and contracts and/or the office of business affairs, the continuing education unit has been vested with the authority to establish a contract with an external constituency in order to offer an institutionally recognized program. Although some flexibility in program delivery is allowed by the gatekeepers of administrative constancy, often misconceptions that flexibility in program services will lessen program quality force the CCC to mimic on-campus norms. Too often, traditional academic culture, accustomed to face-to-face instruction in traditional classroom settings, according to traditional time schedules, blocks attempts by continuing education to use newer delivery formats available through modern technologies, to establish intensive schedules, and to modify student support services so that they can better accommodate working adults.

The challenge in adapting the CCC model in the next era is to assure that academically acceptable, student-responsive collaborations will be developed. What follows is a hypothetical illustration.

> The Coming Wave Corporation contacts a four-year comprehensive public, research-based university, The University of Tradition, with a specific request for a course of instruction designed to help 20 employees learn a state-of-the-art procedure intended to bolster manufacturing potential.
>
> The director of human resources management of the corporation defines the educational need as a graduate-level engineering course (a mutually understood mode of delivery), because 10 of the employees who will attend have bachelor's degrees in engineering and desire graduate-level credit. In addition, there are five employees who do not want university credit but seek relevant information. One of these has a Ph.D. in chemistry; another does not hold an academic degree but expects to find the subject matter relevant to work; and the remaining three possess the prerequisite technical expertise to take the course but would not be able to understand a lecture presented in English. Finally, there are five employees who, although they do not possess the explicit technical background needed to undertake the course, are valued by the corporation and are scheduled for promotion.

In the past, traditional academia has responded to this type of request in any of three ways:

1. Declining to offer the program because the nature of the request is incompatible with the method by which this information has been presented on campus;
2. Acceding to the request, modifying the admission criteria, and potentially endangering the institution's reputation; or
3. Offering a modified solution by eliminating those factors that conflict with academic policy — for example, refusing admission to students who do not meet the explicit course prerequisites.

In this case, the university was asked to offer a graduate course in manufacturing engineering, which could be taken for credit or audit. The continuing education director proposed, based on the work schedules of the potential students, to hold the course at the corporation's headquarters in an intensive weekend format. During the review of the request, the college curriculum committee expressed concern that this modified schedule might decrease academic rigor and quality. However, the engineering faculty eventually approved sponsorship on the grounds that the faculty member who would be teaching the course was well respected and the quality of library resources and computer facilities accessible to students was, in fact, far superior to those available on campus. The only contingency to this approval was that evaluation would be much more rigorous than if the course had been offered on campus. Thus, the continuing educator, as a boundary spanner (Votruba, 1987), collaborated with the academic decision-makers to define a course acceptable to the academy and, in part, responsive to the expressed need.

The second phase of negotiation was then set in motion. The goal of this phase was to identify those employees who would be eligible to take the course under university admission criteria.

At this point the continuing educator, working in conjunction with the admissions office of the engineering college, determined that 12 of the employees met criteria for admission to the course. Yet two groups of employees, those not possessing the requisite level of English comprehension and those lacking the necessary technical expertise, would not be acceptable for admission. After these findings had been confirmed by contact with the potential students, and after consultation with the appropriate university actors, the continuing education director presented a modified proposal to the corporation. The corporation accepted the terms because the proposal met the need of its degreed engineers. However, the company was still faced with the problem of educating two cohorts of employees who did not meet the recognized admission criteria. The company's eventual response to this dilemma was to develop its own training program.

Response to the coming wave. It is anticipated that the CCC model will be used to develop comprehensive strategies by which corporations can educate employees who differ in levels of preparedness. Collaborative programs of employee development will be established, with a broader range of university actors playing a more extensive role in defining educational needs and outcomes. The "canned program," successful in the traditional academic climate, is expected to diminish in importance. The most successful strategies will be those that focus on the learner. A cross-cultural understanding should develop, with faculty and industrial leaders working together for a common educational agenda.

Intra-institutional Contractual Collaboration (ICC) Model

An intra-institutional contractual collaboration (ICC) is a financial model in which two or more academic or administrative entities internal to the university enter into a written working agreement for the development or offering of a program or service. The expertise of each actor is defined in the context of its role and function in the institution. A cost analysis is conducted to determine a fair cost for this defined expertise. Questions of duplication of expertise or service are addressed by leadership according to the policies of recognized governance bodies. The ICC includes an analysis of total costs associated with the delivery of the program or service to new clientele. Funding sources may be internal, external, or a combination of the two.

Vulnerability of the ICC model in the traditional academic context. Frequently, individual academic and administrative units of the university have responded to multidisciplinary needs with completely independent requests for funding. These proposals have often overwhelmed university leadership unaccustomed to managing the pressures from units that function in isolation from, and in competition with, each other. Institutional leadership is bombarded by numerous requests for new funding that reflect little or no communication among units of the same organization. The response of leadership is often similarly isolated, creating, at best, a duplication of effective response mechanisms, and, at worst, a collection of more or less ineffective systems. External actors seeking assistance from the university are confused and overwhelmed when approached by a variety of funding requests emanating from what appears to be a fragmented organization.

The traditional funding allocation process, which is primarily based on competition among units, has created an atmosphere of mistrust within the university. This mistrust lessens, or even eliminates, the potential for collaborative interdisciplinary programming or administrative planning. In addition, the distribution of institutional indirect costs on a general formula basis, rather than on an equity basis typical of the cost center approach, further isolates units. Here is another hypothetical example.

The University of the Metropolis, located in a major geographic center, is experiencing increasing pressure from a variety of citizen and governmental publics to play a more active role in solving problems associated with the public schools. The provost asks the director of continuing education to develop a strategy of response. The director asks the dean of the College of Education to help in this process. The dean agrees to participate.

After several meetings with school officials and elected parent representatives, the director of continuing education and the dean of the college identify several educational needs. These include updating for teachers and administrators and a broad range of coursework for parent leaders. This coursework includes the study of administrative techniques and decision-making, legislative updates, coping with substance abuse and behavioral disorders, and literacy. Effective response on behalf of the university will require support from the College of Education; the departments of mathematics, public administration, political science, communication, and English of the College of Liberal Arts and Sciences; the School of Public Health; the Graduate College; and administrative offices of continuing education, admissions, counseling, and school and college relations.

The use of an ICC in this illustration can enhance both the institutional efficiency and the effectiveness of the university's response. After the educational and administrative needs were defined, appropriate actors of the university were brought together by the director of CE and the dean of the College of Education functioning under the auspices of the provost. This group became the planning team responsible for developing an institutionally acceptable, mutually beneficial response strategy. Each unit identified the capacities it could bring to the response strategy and how it could present a realistic cost projection for implementation. In addition, it identified those elements of the request to which the university was incapable of responding or should not respond because they were inconsistent with the institutional mission.

This example shows how the image of the university as a feudal kingdom, unaccountable in its response to societal needs, can be altered through collaboration among its own internal entities. Furthermore, university leaders insightful enough to encourage cooperative response by providing financial rewards can establish a proactive integrated problem-solving environment.

The continuing education director, who assumes a leadership role in identifying internal strengths and capacities and integrates this activity with a collaborative planning process for course development and presentation, can thereby present a proposal that enhances the efficiency of the process while using the least possible amount of faculty or administrative time and other resources.

Response to the coming wave. To respond effectively, universities must create financial planning strategies that reward collaborative efforts, reduce duplication, and enhance interdisciplinary approaches, especially those addressing major societal needs. Over the past decade, those senior leaders interested solely in encouraging the research productivity of colleges may have relinquished power to individual unit heads. They have created a de facto managerial arena of financial competition characterized by turf quarrels. Although this management mode may have been functional in previous eras, when resources were more plentiful and demands less complicated, it can create havoc when complex multidisciplinary solutions are needed.

Insightful leaders who use innovative financial disbursement mechanisms to respond to new demands can create incentives to both deans and faculty who present collaborative models for program delivery. Such programs streamline services and place a high priority on the transfer of knowledge through innovative, culturally sensitive teaching strategies.

Multi-university Contractual Collaboration (MCC) Model

A multi-university contractual collaboration (MCC) is a written agreement in which two or more recognized providers of the higher education community enter into a formal partnership in which each contributes its special expertise to address a specific societal need through a cooperative educational response. Actors include community colleges, city colleges, public and private colleges, comprehensive research universities, and vocational schools, to name a few. Each member of the collaboration brings to the stage unique programmatic and administrative competencies. In addition, through such a collaboration individual actors reap greater financial benefits than they would have if they had embarked on competing projects in isolation. All direct and indirect costs are included in the contractual negotiations and are covered by externally or internally generated sources, grants, or appropriations.

Vulnerability of the MCC model in the traditional academic context. The concept of consortium arrangements among colleges and universities has existed for several decades, and yet the success rate of these structures is uneven. Several reasons have been suggested, including a lack of mutually acceptable goals, conflicting academic missions, ineffective leadership, power conflicts, differing demands and expectations, and financial competition. Of these, financial competition is perhaps the first issue that needs to be addressed as consortium arrangements are formed. For most institutions, financial survival depends upon generating revenue through enrollments. Therefore, consortium agreements are usually successful only to the degree that each actor is able to generate a level of revenue comparable to the level it would generate if it were not a member of the consortium.

Multi-university collaborations, perhaps more than any other mechanism, will require that an institution evaluate its strengths and its shortfalls, clarify its mission and institutional agenda, and prioritize its uses for resources.

Here is a hypothetical example of such a collaboration:

> In an era of dwindling external resources, five universities and colleges in the same local geographical area offer noncredit programs in management development. These attract employees of several local industries. Each program contains core management seminars, such as time management, as well as some unique content components, such as international negotiation. Three are financially successful, perhaps due to institutional reputation, limited cost, or their close affiliation with alumni responsible for sending employees to the program. Two programs are struggling to maintain solvency. The five institutions, drawn into a consortium agreement by the state governance structure, are asked to create a joint management program. The result is chaotic, with each institution making every effort to undermine the process. Eventually the consortium is disbanded. The two less solvent programs are eliminated in the next year.

Although multi-university collaborations have been advocated for over a decade (Knowles, 1970), especially by legislative governance bodies, the success of any collaboration has been contingent upon common goals, trust, and recognized mutual benefits. Few collaborations survive.

Pragmatically, many institutions that remain isolated may not survive (Levine et al., 1990). The pool of both traditional-age and adult student applicants will decline. Without students, institutions may close their doors. One might argue that this elimination of seemingly superfluous educational providers may in fact benefit society. Yet, with demographic data implying that more diverse educational opportunities will be needed by a growing population of underserved, underprepared citizens, evaluating unique institutional strengths may be a better solution than trying to eliminate redundancy. Levine et al. (1990) emphasize:

The declining number of young people will put institutions of higher education in the position of having to compete for students with the army, an aggressive labor market, and other noncollegiate postsecondary educators. If these competitors are able to maintain their share of the market, then the decline in college enrollments will be even greater than the numbers and population characteristics now indicate. (p. 168)

Although the content of the five programs described in the hypothetical scenario overlapped somewhat, each program contained unique characteristics useful to local industry as it faced the complexities of a new era of competition. Specifically, one of the colleges was well equipped to help industry cope with remedial education needs projected for the work force of the year 2000. Yet these specializations were not considered as strengths when the consortium agreement was terminated.

Response to the coming wave.   In the future, universities must recognize programmatic strengths, realizing that no institution can be a leader in all arenas. An institution that is focused on research may do best to maintain this posture and indeed to expand research-based programs. Yet it may also play a role in providing leadership in planning for collaborative efforts. The critical element in any endeavor, however, is to create financial models that will support unique planning and engender trust.

Bypassing the problems that plagued consortium arrangements of the past, the MCC established under coming wave dynamics will allow institutions to form and reform partnerships based on specific projects. Although the actors may remain constant, the role of each may change as new projects are defined. The MCC will provide a response mechanism that places institutions in formalized limited partnerships rather than loosely defined bureaucratic structures. This should lessen the competition for a dwindling pool of students and limited number of faculty.

No institution, no matter how comprehensive, can serve all future educational needs. However, it can redefine its mission as one in which collaborations with other educational providers are a cornerstone of operations rather than an anomaly.

CULTURAL NORMS AND EXTERNAL EXPECTATIONS: THE EFFECTS ON FINANCE

The coming wave will require of its leadership and its organization a proclivity for learning—learning about the organization's individual strengths and the interconnectedness of its elements. Continuing educators with their long histories of spanning the border between academia and society can contribute a boundary-sensitive perspective consistent with institutional values and external expectations.

Financial planning and budgeting are concepts familiar to continuing education units. The generation of external resources through charging of fees or retention of indirect costs has served continuing education units well in past decades as a means for expanding programs, funding staff, and paying their way in the parent institution. The generation of income, especially in the entrepreneurially oriented continuing education units established at some universities (King & Lerner, 1987), is viewed as the primary indicator of continuing education program or unit success. The final section of this chapter presents issues that must be addressed by leaders of continuing education as they work in managerial relationships with other university decision-makers to develop new financial policies compatible with both academic and societal agendas.

More Than a Cash Cow

The uniqueness of financial planning under new thinking depends on the extent to which university executives and other academic leaders recognize continuing education's ability to support the parent institution by enhancing the institution's image and focusing its mission, as well as providing for its financial survival. Without this broad-based perspective, the fears of some continuing education leadership that the function will fall into a "cash cow" status may be realized (Nicklin, 1991).

Since the early 1980s, even institutions with outstanding records of research and scholarship have experienced increased external pressure to be more "accessible" and provide modified curricula that emphasize applications. Corporations, trying to cope with an ill-prepared work force, have looked to universities to retrain current and future employees. Hospitals, facing shortages in qualified medical professionals, have looked to universities for staff training. In some instances, the mission of the university has matched the practical needs of the external constituencies. In most instances, however, barriers have sprung up as universities have shied away from the training function.

The level of response to new student populations or markets is often financially driven and varies from institution to institution. The populations who are the beneficiaries of greater access are those who most closely match the profile of qualified student defined by admission criteria formulated in past decades, when larger numbers of traditional 18-to-22-year-old students applied for college. The segment of the population receiving the least attention is becoming an ever-growing cohort of underserved. In the coming wave, this cohort will represent the dominant segment of the population. This population, diverse in racial heritage, ethnic background, and age, may need and even demand a variety of support services that enhance retention and graduation. As Levine et al. (1990) have observed, "Restoring the American dream is a national necessity, and today that dream has no more concrete manifestation than attendance at college" (p. 172).

As university leaders find themselves under increasing pressure to address these issues, it is likely that many of them will turn to continuing education for solutions. One hopes these solutions will have broader goals than merely to generate income and will focus on issues of image, mission, and advocacy. Through its many decades of programming and service to unique populations, continuing education, perhaps more than any other unit of the university, is positioned to address these demands.

A Window Rather Than a Wall

In creating a cloistered environment conducive to the generation of new knowledge through research, universities may inadvertently have alienated, and in some instances offended, the private citizens who provide much of the financial support essential for institutional survival. Within this "involvement/detachment paradox" (Lynton, 1984), university leadership has struggled to maintain academic integrity, which depends on the freedom of faculty to create knowledge without considering the practical applications of that knowledge, while responding to numerous, albeit influential publics. Even more symbolic of the alienation are the numerous quasi-universities created by external constituencies, especially those from industry, who became disenchanted when confronted with universities' perceived or real lack of interest in practical applications.

Although the so-called elite institutions have survived the decline in enrollments that followed the graduation of the baby boomers due to their competitive edge in attracting the remaining pool of traditional college-age students and an acceptable cohort of adult learners who possessed similar credentials for admission, this state of affairs is not likely to continue. "Regionally, every portion of the country is going to experience declines in its college-age population through the early 1990s" (Levine et al., 1990, p. 165).

So-called regional or community institutions, which traditionally place a higher value on their teaching and public service missions, may well have an institutional advantage over elite institutions in maintaining financial solvency. During the 1980s, elite institutions tended to respond to declining resource appropriations by eliminating support services and nontraditional delivery modes. Ironically, this forced continuing education organizations to create unique financial models that allowed them to retain revenue generated from external sources. This revenue was then used to support programs and services eliminated under appropriation retrenchment periods.

Strategic Financial Positioning

Outside the mainstream, continuing education created financial strategies that allowed it to meet the exigencies of traditional appropriation processes. This quality of "adaptiveness" (Simerly & Associates, 1987) may contribute to the future survival of the institution. While traditional academia maintained the traditional office hours and traditional classroom schedules that had suited the nonworking, residential students of the 1950s, continuing education instituted weekend colleges, "in-house" programs, student services offices, and payment by credit card. Locally held accounts were developed under legislative audit guidelines that gave continuing education the authority to collect fees and pay direct and indirect program costs. All this took place under a system parallel to the traditional funding mechanisms of the university.

Fiscal accountability for the management of these mechanisms rested with continuing education directors. Internal and external audits, including systems for carrying over balances for future program development and administration, became a component of the entrepreneurial financial management strategies established by creative continuing education leaders. Today continuing education, prepared with fiscally responsible systems and strategies, can provide the university as a whole with a model for flexible response to demands of the coming wave.

Dynamic Leadership

Will university leadership recognize the resource it possesses in continuing education in the coming wave? Even without a crystal ball one can anticipate that levels of advocacy will vary in accordance with the level of vision of senior leadership. Those leaders described by Sashkin (1988) as "visionary" possess broader cognitive capabilities, which enable them to assimilate and evaluate numerous variables necessary to higher-level problem-solving. Those leaders possessing both visionary and survival instincts may begin their problem-solving by looking inward and thereby discovering the continuing education unit as an untapped resource capable of responding to diverse demands.

Like Sashkin, Simerly et al. (1987) emphasize the importance of strategic planing as a means for strengthening leadership. They note: "At a time when the national consciousness of the need for organizational excellence has never been higher, a central issue has become how to integrate effective planning into leadership activities" (p. 1). Coming wave leadership, faced with declining resources and increased demands for accountability, will need to develop organizational strategies that lessen the impacts of departmental ownership by instilling a type of organizational culture that rewards collaborative efforts focused on addressing coming wave priorities.

Faculty Rewards and Expectations

As we prepare to meet the future, we know that a limited number of the full-time faculty who have enjoyed the "real-world" experience of teaching adult learners will be strong allies. In practice, only the most gifted researchers/teachers can meet the expectations of adult learners. Cross's (1981) research into faculty and student expectations reinforces this truth, known to every experienced continuing education director. Adult students, if they are dissatisfied with a faculty member, will convey their dissatisfaction in a variety of ways, including withdrawal of financial support for the program and perhaps for the institution. "Adults must feel competent, exhibit confidence during learning and feel at ease in the learning environment" (Viechnicki, Bohlin, & Milheim, 1990, p. 13).

The ongoing discussion of the degree to which faculty should modify teaching strategies to accommodate diverse learning needs is addressed by numerous researchers (Cross, 1981; Knox, 1981; Eble & McKeachie, 1986; Brookfield, 1990). However, from a fiscal standpoint, continuing education directors know that successful faculty are those who retain academic credibility while adapting their teaching styles. Those continuing education directors who neglect to consider this when selecting faculty members and planning marketing strategies (Campbell, 1990) soon find enrollments dwindling and financial planning an impossibility. Adult learners expect fine teaching.

From the faculty member's viewpoint, continuing education can provide a mechanism whereby dwindling salaries can be bolstered through "overload" compensation mechanisms. Although one might assume that these mechanisms would stimulate faculty involvement in external teaching, in many instances the opposite occurs. Legislative budgeting processes often prohibit the inclusion of enrollment "headcount" for courses where additional compensation is given to the faculty member. Therefore, departments reap no tangible reward. As a result, faculty—especially the young and untenured—are discouraged from, and often penalized for, teaching above the acceptable load.

Many faculty members who advocate continuing education as a valid organizational function find it more productive to work "out of sight," apart from the system. In practice, these Robin Hoods of university tradition take nothing from the university; on the contrary, they contribute the intangibles of prestige and external visibility, valuable assets in the coming wave.

SUMMARY

The coming wave confronts institutions of higher education with a financial dilemma: how to maintain academic rigor and integrity while responding to an increasingly diverse population that does not fit the traditional model of the past decades. This dilemma must be faced amid a flood of financial decline and a storm of increased demands. This chapter suggests that the continuing education function, with its history of embracing flexible yet academically viable solutions to new and unique educational needs, is a means to enhance university effectiveness in the face of the coming wave.

REFERENCES

Bennis, W., & Nanus, B. (1985). *Leaders: The strategies for taking charge*. New York: Harper & Row.

Brookfield, S. D. (1990). *The skillful teacher*. San Francisco: Jossey-Bass.

Campbell, M. D. (1990). Building participation through market research. *The Guide Series*. Urbana, IL: University of Illinois at Urbana-Champaign.

Cross, K. P. (1981). *Adults as learners: Increasing participation and facilitating learning*. San Francisco: Jossey-Bass.

Dahl, D. A. (1980). Resources. In A. B. Knox & Associates (Eds.), *Developing, administering and evaluating adult education* (pp. 154–180). San Francisco: Jossey-Bass.

Deal, T. E. (1987). Building an effective organizational culture: How to be community-oriented in a traditional institution. In R. G. Simerly & Associates (Eds.), *Strategic planning and leadership in continuing education* (p. 89). San Francisco: Jossey-Bass.

DiBiaggio, J. A. (1987). The Legacy: Serving the world, the people and the ideas of America's state and land-grant universities. Proceedings of the National Association of State Universities Land Grant Colleges. Washington, DC.

Donaldson, J. F. (1990). Managing credit programs in continuing higher education. *The Guide Series*. Urbana, IL: University of Illinois Press.

Eble, K. E., & McKeachie, W. J. (1986). *Improving undergraduate education through faculty development*. San Francisco: Jossey-Bass.

Edelson, P. J. (1990, Winter). Campus cultures and continuing higher education: Discovering relationships. *Continuing Higher Education Review, 54*(1), 35–42.

King, B. K., & Lerner, A. W. (1987, Autumn). Organizational structure and performance dynamics in continuing education administration. *Continuing Higher Education Review*, *51*(3), 21–38.

Knowles, M. S. (1970). *The modern practice of adult education: Andragogy versus pedagogy*. New York: Associated Press.

Knox, A. B. (1981). The continuing education agency and its parent organization. In J. C. Votruba (Ed.), *New directions for continuing education* (No. 9) (pp. 1–11). San Francisco: Jossey-Bass.

Levine, A., & Associates. (1990). *Shaping higher education's future, demographic realities and opportunities 1990–2000*. San Francisco: Jossey-Bass.

Lynton, E. A. (1984). *The missing connection between business and the universities*. New York: Macmillan.

Lynton, E. A., & Elman, S. E. (1987). *New priorities for the university*. San Francisco: Jossey-Bass.

Matkin, G. W. (1985). *Effective budgeting in continuing education*. San Francisco: Jossey-Bass.

Nicklin, J. L. (1991, May). As enrollment in continuing education booms, some fear programs will be used as cash cows. *The Chronicle of Higher Education*, pp. 1, A31.

Sashkin, M. (1988). The visionary leader. In J. A. Conger, Kanungo, R. N., & Associates, *Charismatic leadership* (pp. 122–160). San Francisco: Jossey-Bass.

Simerly, R. G., & Associates. (1987). *Strategic planning and leadership in continuing education*. San Francisco: Jossey-Bass.

Strand, D. R. (1990). Continuing education: Defining the missions of AASCU institutions. American Association of State Colleges and Universities. Journal booklet, pp. 96–103.

Viechnicki, K. J., Bohlin, R. M., & Milheim, W. D. (1990, Fall). Instructional motivation of adult learners: An analysis of student perceptions of continuing education. *The Journal of Continuing Higher Education*, *38*, 10–14.

Votruba, J. C. (1987). From marginality to mainstream: Strategies for increasing internal support for continuing education. In R. Simerly (Ed.), *Strategic planning and leadership in continuing education* (pp. 185–201). San Francisco: Jossey-Bass.

Winters, R. O. (1991, May). Mainstreaming: Blessing or curse for continuing education professionals? *Five Minutes with ACHE*, pp. 1–4.

7

Setting the Norms for Coming Wave Relationships: Continuing Education and External Organizations

Allan W. Lerner

This chapter makes the point that a major feature of the coming wave in continuing higher education is the need for highly skilled educational leadership at the boundary between the mega-university and its external environment of other organizational actors. For a variety of reasons on both sides, the mega-universities and their external organizational networks will feel the need to intensify their relationships. This chapter suggests that the mega-universities would be well-advised to establish the norms of this relationship in ways that protect their institutional interests, and that if they fail to do so, the norms that develop are likely to be adverse to their interests in several respects.

The chapter begins by outlining some of the signs of, and reasons for, the increased interaction between the universities and their organizational environments. A model of the stages of their interaction is suggested for heuristic purposes. The strategic interests of the mega-universities at each stage of the model are considered. The pitfalls in the relationship at various stages are also examined. Throughout consideration of these issues, the unique capacity of continuing education as a functional priority and a structural tool in developing external relations is explained. In the process, the notion of the "trainication mindset," an indicator of the confusion between the educational mission and the training role, is given considerable attention. So too is consideration given to the concept of "high-reliability organization," a model of organizational hyperperformance which, it will be suggested, is an axis along which the mega-university will have to redirect itself in response to coming wave demands.

MEGA-UNIVERSITIES AND EXTERNAL ORGANIZATIONS: MUTUAL ATTRACTION

The last several years have seen an explosion of literature on both public- and private-sector productivity. Whether upbeat or alarmist, such works emphasize the importance of transforming organizational cultures by removing obstacles to increased productivity and by unleashing the excellence that allegedly is waiting to pounce on mediocrity and devour it (see Morley, 1986; Ouchi, 1982; Peters & Waterman, 1982; Stewart, 1989; Volker, 1989).

The universities have become major sources of expertise on the understanding of, and intervention in, so-called organizational cultures. Unlike the anthropologists of old, who took great pains to leave no traces of their presence in the cultural environments they observed, modern organizational scholars are eager to offer their assistance to errant organizational cultures and to leave a therapeutic mark. The attractiveness of increasing organizational performance by soliciting the sage intervention of culture consultants has not been lost on the leaders of large-scale organizations, and so the universities are increasingly sought out as sources of assistance in putting organizations aright. Through their faculties in management, public administration, industrial psychology, psychiatry, and related fields, and in specific content areas that form the core technologies of given client organizations, universities have broadened their assistance to external organizational clients, increasingly lending an interorganizational dimension to what were formerly freelanced professorial consultantships and applied research projects undertaken in isolation.

Clearly, this trend must by judged, on the whole, to be good, as well as irreversible. The use of knowledge enhances its social value, and its testing in applied circumstances refines it.

At the same time, the increasingly broad interests of large, modern mega-universities are associated with growing university dependence on policy and opinion networks that extend beyond their traditional clienteles. Thus, when universities can strengthen their interorganizational relationships by leading with what they do best — their faculty's teaching and research, and public-service projects stemming from that research — then both the universities and their relationship partners are well served.

It is in the nature of "changing cultures" to require "organizational intervention," and it is in the nature of intervention to provide education for practical organizational living. With T-groups, management forums, leadership seminars, executive development workshops, management training programs, certificate programs, social marketing studies, professional training workshops, and the like frequently serving as the media of choice for consultant involvement in client organizations, the universities are providing expert manpower for a burgeoning industry: organizational competitiveness services. When they do this as a matter of institutional policy and with strategic institutional interests, the universities also transform activities formerly undertaken independently, by their employees, into policy instruments serving interinstitutional agendas.

It is a natural and, arguably, an inevitable product of market forces in a crowded field that relationships between organizational clients and expert consultants are being consolidated with increasing frequency into relationships between organizational clients and the universities that house the consulting professoriate. Even when university-level interests are not explicitly recognized as being involved in faculty and departmental dealings with external actors, intermediate-level systemic interests—departmental, say, or interdepartmental ones—are often acknowledged to be affected. In the interest of improving planning, control, and visibility, reducing liability, and consolidating individual-level interests, it is natural that some aggregate centralizing level of institutional legitimacy will be invoked in the working-through of relationships between university citizens and outsiders. This is so even when the executive levels of the institutions involved have yet to incorporate such activities formally into their own strategic visions.

Through name-association alone, continuing education will be tapped with increasing frequency as a valuable part of the administrative tool kit for developing and maintaining such relationships. Often this will be done by middle-level actors ambitiously pursuing middle-level agendas, in many cases ahead of their institutional leaders' directives and on the strength of proactive interpretation of ambiguous, general philosophies of mission. The latter only vaguely indicate the parameters of middle-level action in universities. We are entering an era in which the moonlighting professor clandestinely pursuing a consulting relationship with an external client will be increasingly replaced by triangular relations among faculty, external organizations, and academic institutions.

The question is whether the executive leadership of universities and external organizations will adapt their strategic outlooks to absorb, and make full use of, the interinstitutional linkages that entrepreneurial middle-level actors are establishing among themselves. Continuing education in the coming wave will be a central actor in this process, as a natural focus of middle-level, de facto linkages, or as a strategic tool of executive leadership, depending on the foresight of the latter. The professionalized, mega-institutional service society of the coming decades will likely involve an increasingly crowded field of interorganizational relations characterized by fluid but complex networks. Where networks include universities, continuing education, a boundary actor by virtue of mission, resource access, and personnel, will be a node at which interorganizational relations first form. Where university executives understand this, the process will be strategically influenced. Where they do not, the process will be haphazard, fathomable only through the middle-level agendas of the middle-level actors, a level of micro knowledge that few executives normally acquire inadvertently.

The formation of such interorganizational networks is in essence a "natural," unplanned process. Let us call it "functional corporatization," to signify the elaboration of complex organizational patterns around a skeletal process already in place among simpler organizational units. De facto complexes of interorganizational functioning will follow the systematically natural, informal ways of easily "getting things done" from the common-denominator perspective of the middle-level actors involved. Such functional corporatization has its benefits and its costs. Middle-level actors, like all calculating actors, will seek to maximize the benefits and minimize the costs from their own perspectives. However, what is desirable at the middle level is not necessarily desirable at the strategic level, where many middle-level interests must be homogenized and then weighed against purely executive-level interests to produce an institutional-level strategy, if one is ever developed.

For university executives not content to have their institutions led amoeba-like by surges from various middle-level points, the first challenge will be to think through the strategic and tactical issues involved in putting relations with external clients on an institutionally sound footing capable of supporting a multidimensional but strategically controlled university agenda. The trick in achieving this for an inherently loosely coupled institution such as a university is to constructively co-opt and softly shape initiatives that spring from the middle level. Continuing education will be a major source of middle-level development. Thus, embracing new uses of continuing education can be, if nothing else, a way of acting early to shape the particulars of the inevitable. Such a strategic choice can serve senior administrators well. The burden will then be on them to educate their external relationship partners regarding the mutual benefits of interaction through the continuing education medium.

These other actors in the system are more likely to think they know what they want from a university than they are likely to know how to get it, and are not likely to understand the university's needs, workings, or interests as well as the university understands the external actor. The university is likely to be more loosely linked than its prospective relationship partners. It will benefit from educating such organizational counterparts to approach it through those university access points that will facilitate their access to the knowledge resources existing within the university. These access points can be mobilized when new interorganizational partners present themselves. The university must educate external organizations to approach it at the points where the university will find it easiest to absorb the approach, and begin to focus conceptual and material resources for a response. Executive levels within the university must know where these points are, how they operate, what they need to operate best, and how to collaborate with them internally in strategically appropriate responses.

Given that continuing education will be a prime access point, the key conceptual questions at the continuing education node would seem to be the following:

1. What kind of relationship should exist between universities and the corporations and government agencies that seek to draw on faculty expertise to improve the productivity of their organizations and reform their organizational cultures?
2. How should the relationship between a university (through its faculty) and an external organization be shaped? How should the university move toward such a relationship, and is complete individual latitude for its faculty appropriate in that process?
3. What are the foreseeable tendencies, on either side of the institutional relationship, to smother lofty aspirations with mediocrity, either by chronic smallmindedness on the part of executives or by faculty's willingness to settle for quick success from a short-term, self-interested perspective?

To develop answers to these questions that can serve as orienting principles for forging successful relationships with external organizational actors though the continuing education portal, universities must understand what their relevant strengths and weaknesses are. In principle, universities are capable of assisting external organizations on four dimensions:

1. Training of personnel;
2. Education of personnel;
3. Research on specific problems that lead external organizations to contact the universities for assistance; and
4. Sharing in the creation of an active, continuously functioning practitioner-academic community that provides an atmosphere of mutual support and intellectual stimulation beyond specific projects, programs, and spin-off ventures.

The four dimensions represent levels of increasing sophistication in organization-university relations. It seems useful, then, to view the development of an ideal relationship between a university and an organization new to each other as a movement through these four stages of a relationship-building process. Continuing education is well suited as a vehicle for the crucial early stages of the relationship.

As a developmental model, the four-stage process noted above may not apply universally. There is variety among the actual cases of interorganizational relationship-building between universities and external organizations. For example, one can easily understand how individuals moving to new university or organizational positions, and bringing their experiences, network associations, and conclusions with them, may move to establish relationships with institutional counterparts on one or another of these dimensions without recreating all the prior stages of the model relationship. Indeed, the frequency of academic, corporate, and governmental mobility within and across such organizational groupings should not be underestimated. Similarly, for many reasons, relationships may not always move through all stages, or completely through a given stage. Furthermore, the enactment of any stage may entail activities of considerable or modest scope. Additionally, activities at any given level may expand to involve multiple participants drawn from government, corporation, and third-sector entities at one or several internal levels, and participants from one or several levels within the university community.

While these subtleties are to be expected, it is nonetheless important to begin the conceptualization process by analyzing the generic stages of organization-university interaction. The empirical quirks and lags of relationship development would seem to represent variations in the basic process.

If we first define each of these four stages of relationship and discuss the opportunities as well as the pitfalls associated with each, we can then elaborate the appropriateness of continuing education formats to developing successful relationships at each level.

THE FIRST AND SECOND DIMENSIONS: TRAINING AND EDUCATION

Experience suggests that a common problem in government agencies' and non-profit organizations' contacts with academic programs (and with universities' continuing education offices) is the client organizations' failure to distinguish between training and education. This is not a matter of mere definition. Frequently, it portends a resurfacing of the problems that have often brought such organizations to the university in the first place.

Training should be thought of as a relatively specific, narrow, programmatically noncontroversial, technical process of communicating the information and drilling the skills necessary to perform routine activities. To be trained is to be taught to do a specific task. The activity may be extremely useful and socially important, but it remains a body of routine techniques.

In contrast, *educating* should be thought of as building the intellect, broadly construed to include the maturing of values. To educate people is to lead them to think differently and more sophisticatedly regarding a certain field of knowledge—but inevitably also to think more sophisticatedly in general, as the educated mind begins to continuously educate itself and reshape its perspective (see Ahn & Saint-Germain, 1988; Schott, 1986; Wolf, 1983).

Thus, one can be trained to use a new personnel procedure, but one must be educated to think about personnel matters in a new and more sophisticated way. One can be trained to write more clearly, but must be educated in order to develop more insightful things to write. One can be trained to organize one's desk and calendar, but must be educated to develop more mature priorities and programs in which to invest one's time. One can be trained in routine tactics, but must be educated to think strategically.

Considerable practical implications flow from this distinction. For one thing, university faculty and most university programs are generally geared to educate rather than to train. On the other hand, large external organizations tend to have training or "educational" offices, which are generally geared to train rather than to educate, euphemisms notwithstanding.

In graduate professional programs, where the intention is to produce well-prepared practitioners, some attention is always given to training issues. This, however, is not the programs' major emphasis, and when training is the matter at hand, it is always in the context of a broader educational goal. The creation of "clinical faculty" may be understood in this context as an attempt to resolve the tension between training and education pressures by developing an intermediate category.

As interventions in organizational cultures and the creation of a climate of "excellence" and "leadership" are invariably seen as the prerequisites for a qualitative improvement in organizational life, university consultants are frequently solicited to offer programs that trainers have been reluctant to offer, or have failed in their attempts to offer (in executives' eyes, if not their own). It is to the universities that organizations often turn next, albeit still in search of "better training."

Even "training" as such, in some components of universities' graduate programs, however, often focuses on an interesting hypothetical case rather than an immediate practical one; on a historical case that illustrates an educational point—a case *of* something, rather than a current case selected to test proficiency. In the main, universities are best at educating and are less interested in, and less adept at, training. This distinction is fundamental to continuing education in the coming wave. Continuing education will continue to offer both training and education, but it must not confuse the goals, requirements, evaluation criteria, and relationship value of the two. The university cannot afford to spoil contacts by failing to identify genuine needs and interests, even on the part of external organizations that fail to see their own enlightened interests at first. Also, the university cannot afford to misdirect or misuse its human and material resources. Competing institutions will now be ready, in a tighter, shared field, to gain from such mistakes. Mistakes are easy to make in the development of interorganizational relationships.

The first point where things can go wrong in the development of new training programs for employees is in the initial contact. This contact can be made by either side, though usually it is made by the organization. The external organization's contact and follow-up people are often training division personnel. Senior administrators may be involved in early meetings, but usually think and operate in the language of their own training division, on which they rely for orientation in dealing with university representatives at this first level of the relationship, and in whose language they develop and maintain internal support for program ventures on this dimension. The underdeveloped language of initial contact actually constitutes a mindset, which, for our purposes, may be referred to as the "trainication" mindset.

The trainication mindset and its associated language are frequently characterized by lip service to the value of education per se, combined with actual preferences for quick, allegedly objective evidence of a program's impact as measured through self-reporting by participants and the tone of a nonthreatening "briefing" or "updating" encounter with strong social overtones. The goal of organizational clients is to "change the culture," or "upgrade performance," albeit quickly, painlessly, and without any self-examination by the organizational leadership. Like analysands in the psychotherapeutic relationship, these clients often "just want the answer," hoping to avoid the process of getting that answer.

The language of the trainication mindset often includes frequent references to the general value of education. However, implicitly or explicitly, the criteria for judging an attractive trainication program reveal that in reality more emphasis is being placed on training. Such criteria include supervisor selection of candidates based on agency-standardized screening; marathon workday sessions; short, intense formats; a crisp list of vaguely conceptualized objectives in a pseudo-operations language; program evaluation (rating) forms that are administered daily and filled out in class by employees attending the programs; emphasis on written handout materials; quick issuance of certificates of completion or agency certifications of some sort; small-groups formats; industrial training–style audiovisual elements, and related props and devices.

The problem with consumerist trainication priorities on the part of clients is that such priorities inhibit the necessary moderate frustration, the suspension of control, the willing vulnerability, the commitment to patience that are the prerequisites for being educated. These qualities are required of those entering an intellectual relationship, in this case with the professor as senior partner and the university as senior organization.

Programs that are worthwhile by the standards of training and education may or may not be fully appreciated and accurately assessed when viewed from the trainication perspective. Normally, in a training program, would-be students who are adequately prepared should make satisfactory progress as a group, progress being, of course, defined in light of the group's entering proficiencies. Satisfactoriness will be defined in light of the intensity and duration of the training format chosen. Normally, in an educational program, preparedness is harder to determine. However, the ability to produce insights, analytical presentations, and projects can be assessed over time—the key in educational programs—and can be roughly gauged through comparison with participants' early efforts, or through students' self-reports of increased understanding, or through peers', superiors', or even subordinates' observations of positive change in the quality of participant performance, behavior, general contributions to the group, and leadership.

It is the cumulative effect of such successes at the individual and group levels that eventually transforms an organization. This is a hard lesson, not a salesman's message, and cannot be easily conveyed unless one can also show an understanding of the inner world of the particular client organization. Continuing education personnel working in tandem with the appropriate faculty consultants are less threatening, more credible and appropriate conveyors of such messages than are general university administrators in the early relationship with new organizational contacts.

Breaking the Trainication Mindset with Continuing Education

Continuing education units, located as they are at the university boundary with the external world of organizational clients, can and should be educationally and organizationally bicultural. Thus, they are in an excellent position to nip the trainication mindset in the bud, provided continuing education is granted the status of translator and consultant to both parties in the crucial early discussions of the manifest agenda that brings them together. Much is at stake in these early encounters. In the coming wave environment, universities can no longer afford to waste these opportunities.

Universities wishing to build broad and deep relationships with external organizations would thus do well to lead with continuing education programs and properly selected and trained continuing education personnel in the early stages of such relationships. These early stages are vulnerable to derailment amid the effort to disengage the client from the trainication mindset.

The trainication mindset is evaluation-centered, but more from a consumerist than an analytical perspective. The consumerist perspective relies unduly on the students' omniscience in even the earliest stages of program, thus reversing with a vengeance the normal evaluational relationship between instructor and student. This outlook may often be largely attributable to a group anxiety about reentering the student position, which leads to the defensive posture of valued customer, if not patron. All program benefits are then measured in terms of their immediate impact on work performance. Training and education are viewed as an interpersonal process rather than an internal, individual process. Generally the trainication mindset resists thoughtful assessment of the value of training and education programs in light of realistic and appropriate expectations suited to the format, students, scope of subject, and prevailing academic and professional understanding of the difficulties to be expected in training people in a particular technology or moving them to a certain level of conceptual and intellectual sophistication.

In any event, when a program has been judged positively from a trainication point of view, there is often an immediate inclination to widen participation in the program by scheduling the piloted material for ever-larger agency audiences. In traditionally led continuing education units with a heavily entrepreneurial bent, emphasis on a high volume of short-term programming may abet this client tendency.

The limitation of this approach is that it stifles the maturation of university-client relations through higher levels. As volume of participation is emphasized, the audiences tend to become increasingly heterogeneous in terms of unit orientation within the agency, level of experience, and hierarchical position. Thus, the obstacles to genuinely educating may actually increase, as education deteriorates into entertainment and a student body deteriorates into a mere audience. It is not only a continuing education unit's interest, but is arguably its pedagogic responsibility to stress the importance of avoiding—or at least not euphemistically mislabeling—such educational deteriorations, not only by pointing out their pedagogic limitations but also *by indicating the lost opportunities for richer university-external organization relations that such transformations represent*, because of the immaturity they foster in would-be-partner organizations.

University units at some institutions may rush to cooperate in these situations in the hope of securing short-term benefits. These benefits can include visibility in the agency community as well as in the university community (though the benefits of such internal visibility are sometimes genuine and sometimes imagined). Universities in the coming era who wish, as a deliberate policy objective, to confine continuing education units to narrowly entrepreneurial agendas, may of course do so and be happy with the result. Educational ethics issues remain wherever the internal or external labeling of an activity is unclear. But, presuming truth in rationalization, there is nothing wrong with offering intellectualized entertainment at worst, or narrow training at best, provided all concerned understand what is happening.

Continuing education units beginning dealings with external client organizations should be aware that these organizations frequently behave seemingly inconsistently because of anxieties on the part of their own training division personnel. These individuals understandably fear at first that their function is being contracted out.

The consequence is that relationships between agencies and universities that could rise beyond trainication have a high mortality rate, because agency executives interested in a broader and more mature caliber of program from the university must now face internal sensitivities. These concern the prospect of cultivating relationships that appear to introduce inefficiencies by duplicating in-house capabilities. In such circumstances, it is continuing education administrators whose mission allows them to follow the subtleties in specific organization-university relationships to the point of being able to diagnose and treat the outbreak of such resistance as part of a team that includes the participating faculty. This is a critical function of continuing education in the era of the coming wave.

Graduate professional degree programs are a burgeoning component of the senior university's curriculum. This presumably reflects an underlying societal trend toward professionalizing social roles in service economies (Lerner, 1976a, 1976b; Lopata, 1976; Shapiro, 1985). University faculty and administrators of professional programs and units with a mission that includes serving the current needs of the practitioner community are professionally committed to fostering contact with practitioner groups such as government agencies and professionalized corporations. Faculty themselves are often insufficiently aware of their own positions on the training-educating continuum and are thus also vulnerable to adapting to, rather than breaking, the client's trainication mindset.

Consequently, a common outcome of first contacts is an agreement to deliver program content that defers to the trainication mindset. This may be done in the hope of transcending that mindset, but, wishful thinking aside, such efforts often deteriorate into struggles to meet trainication's stylistic criteria. A university outreach program can thus become trapped in trainication, or "fail" to meet its objectives, eventually settling into a rut, until the program is terminated by either side.

A very common type of trainication program is the series of one-day workshops on topics such as leadership, decision-making, time management, supervisory skills, and/or motivation. *There is nothing inherently wrong or wasteful about such workshop series.* From the perspective of this chapter, however, failure to clarify the difference between training and education when determining how to teach such subjects in a workshop format renders the workshop's purposes, potentials, and limits hopelessly problematic.

Training on any of these topics entails approaching them at a narrow, operational level. For example, one cannot "train" someone in decision-making. One can, however, spend a day on various narrow but useful computational, procedural techniques in current use that serve decision-makers who generally already understand what they are doing and do not need, or at this moment do not wish, to explore broader issues of the decision-making process and its relationship to agency and unit organization and function.

However, when university assistance is sought out of a need to improve the quality of decision-making and decision-maker awareness and thinking because "things are not what they should be" in a given unit or agency, a day or two spent on a little of this or that specific technique is utterly useless. (At the same time, the trainication mindset is often more comfortable with such content, perhaps because this content can be ostensibly "evaluated" from a generalist, even lay, frame of reference.)

To continue with this example, such a case would seem to require educational work to develop an awareness of a deeper-rooted problem behind the feeling that things are not what they should be, and to develop the insight and analytical ability needed to reflect on such issues individually and collectively. At the same time, where a fundamental problem does not exist, and where well-functioning decision-makers need training in particular techniques that are appropriate and available, but not fully utilized in their work practices, *training* in decision-making is of course entirely appropriate. The important issue is that the distinction between training and education must be understood, and that euphemism and confusion must not be allowed to obscure the distinction, because the proper use of resources, chances for significant results, and healthy agency university relationship-building all depend on a mature grasp of the issues rising from this distinction.

To illustrate further, education regarding organizational decision-making will at first avoid discussion of technique issues, and focus instead on the generic aspects of agency decision-making processes, the interplay between routinization and deliberate decision-making, operation by nondecision, and the group and unit dynamics of decision-making processes, probing for the implicit rules of decision-making behavior in the unit, for formulation, implementation, and evaluation issues inherent in decision-making processes generally and at the agency, and so on. In short, the initial focus is on the broader context of decision-making rather than the mechanics of the process or the choice and use of techniques.

Another important concern is that programs with genuinely educational goals cannot readily be presented in a short-format (one- or two-day) workshop. To the contrary, they are best presented through continuous management seminars, possibly held on-site, and with a special emphasis on the agency context. These programs are decidedly not amenable to quick pay-off or daily assessment of results via participant rating forms.

It cannot be overstressed that participants in educational programs must consent to being intellectually strip-searched as part of the process, however tactfully, empathically, supportively, and respectfully that may be done. It is in providing this level of assistance that university faculty come into their own.

In the era of the coming wave, it is incumbent upon the modern university to deal with the environment, rather than retreat from it. That relationship must be developed from a position of certainty about the university's core values. Communicating those values at the educational boundary with the external organizational environment is a task highly suited to an office of continuing education, by virtue of its administrative definition and natural function.

Many experienced university faculty are quite capable of providing a useful workshop experience from the educating rather than training perspective. Administrative authentication of this view is needed to bolster the credibility of the would-be educator of external clients who will communicate this position, thereby deflating the client's trainication expectations. Continuing education administrators in co-development and liaison roles are in an excellent position to lend such administrative authentication when dealing with external client contacts.

Certainly, disabusing potential external clients of their notions about the feasibility and desirability of trainication programs is a task that requires both scholarly and administrative efforts. The posture of the professor will always be different from that of the trainer. For example, when a professor conducts a workshop on decision-making, the professor will inevitably, because of students' preconceptions about the professorial role, serve as a symbol, a model, in addition to conveying a narrow, particular content message. At the same time, the professor may be expected to approach such a subject not by formulaic drilling in narrow techniques but by communicating through the workshop format that sophistication in decision-making begins with attaining analytical prowess as a prerequisite to the acquisition of procedural techniques. This is sufficient to loosen audience thinking and stimulate some internal reassessment of perspective. However, it will not directly affect short-term behavior in existing work routines.

Such outcomes run contrary to the expectations of the trainication mindset. As a result, it is necessary to establish at the outset that the would-be client will accept such an educational program and such educational goals in place of trainication expectations. The task requires the partnership of the professor and the administrator, together representing pedagogic and institutional philosophy. This team of educator and continuing education administrator is the vital proactive unit in the successful performance of the continuing education function in the coming wave era.

These observations would hold true for other frequently requested trainication programs, such as those in the fields of motivation and leadership. In contrast, requests for trainication programs in stress management, time management, and supervision practices, and, of course, requests for training in the use of statistical packages for microcomputers, in spreadsheets, in new technological practices specific to particular professional fields, and so on, are more properly requests for training. As indicated earlier, continuing education programs of this type can be successful as such. Even here, however, conceptual clarity is important, and a credible team of scholar and institutional administrative representatives is invaluable in orienting the representatives of external organizations to the task at hand.

Practical Implications for Fostering University-Agency Training and Education Relationships

Several practical implications follow from the preceding discussion. First, the absolutely indispensable prerequisite in the early stages of healthy agency-university relations is that considerable time—over several meetings, if necessary—be spent on (a) hammering home the distinction between training and education; (b) carefully and thoroughly diagnosing what agencies *need*, taking what they *say* only as raw data in the diagnostic process; (c) carefully assessing the university's *training* capabilities in specific areas, in contrast to its *educating* capabilities; (d) insisting on the active involvement of agency executives or executive staff in the diagnostic phase, in addition to the presence of training division personnel; (e) clearly establishing the relationship between educational and/or training objectives, the format to be used, the results to be expected, and the appropriate measures for assessing results, and (f) the relationship between the agency interests in training and/or education, its long-term expectations for work-force segments, and agency/organizational aspirations for overall performance in various functional areas.

Continuing education administrators in the coming wave will have to be capable of acting as a liaison—between client and university, between client and professor, and at times between university and professor—in relationships such as the one described. Otherwise, continuing education will be drowned by the demands of the new wave, with either of two institutional consequences: (a) powerful, socially vital relationships between universities and external organizations will frequently not be developed where they could be, or (b) university units with narrower agendas and perspectives will form the relationships that do develop, frequently curtailing them to fit their own more limited vision, or distorting their emphasis to fit extraneous or even counterproductive interests from the institution's perspective.

Given that most senior university faculties educate rather than train, the best role for the university in the training process may often be that of educating the trainers—the in-house training division staff. The trainers will train best if they have received the material they pass on in an educational context.

To illustrate, public agencies with a heavy volume of street-level, walk-in contact with clientele often desire to improve the interpersonal tone and procedural efficiency of contact with clients at the public counter, in terms of say, client satisfaction, accuracy of information-gathering, and accuracy of referral decisions and subsequent tracking of client movements throughout various units of the agency depending on the categorizations and decisions made at the public counter. There are clear parallels in the private sector regarding customers.

Trainers are best at training employees in such specific in-house procedures, which an external organization will establish for itself. Professors are best at educating trainers in the psychology of training, in explaining models that describe and predict the behavior of so-called street-level bureaucrats (or salespeople or other organizational representatives), and in explaining the factors that determine the effectiveness of various techniques associated with trainers' roles. These can include the analysis of work flow across units in terms of patterns tending to exaggerate or ameliorate bottlenecks created by errors at the public counter, and so on. The trainer, having been thus educated, can then endeavor to improve standing procedures taught in the training programs.

Similarly, many public agencies and private organizations have developed motivation programs associated with employee orientation programs.

Faculty are rarely suited to conduct these orientation programs. However, they are well suited to make sure that trainers know what they are talking about when they seek to communicate the underlying meaning of in-house philosophies or programs of motivation, or when they describe universal hierarchies of needs, needs for mentors and models, needs for participation, and so on, which have become the stuff of management manuals circulated within large agencies. This understanding of how a university's major resource, its faculty, should by utilized in educational relationships with external organizations is an indispensable element in the success of university-organizational relationships. One of continuing education's future functions will be to promote this understanding both within the university and outside it.

It follows that universities should wholeheartedly advocate the delivery of educational programs to public agencies and private organizations in need of them. However, universities must be careful to educate the agency representatives in the relationship between educational objectives and appropriate formats. In this regard, the university community must discipline itself to offer sound advice based on clear thinking about the advantages and drawbacks of various formats. Continuing education units will first have to educate their own parent organizations in this area.

If the relationship between objectives and formats is not clarified, entrepreneurial zeal on a university's part can often lead to hasty commitments and thereafter to inconsistent behavior at the expense of solid results and long-term credibility with clientele, and ultimately at the expense of scholarly credibility.

An example from my experience at my own institution will illustrate the point. I have taught—under the auspices of the University of Illinois at Chicago's (UIC) master's program in public administration, which offers an accredited professional degree; through the administrative structure of the Office of Continuing Education; and with the cooperation of my parent academic department—for several years at, variously, a government agency, two government hospitals, and at a major federal agency's facilities. These programs entailed a year-long, credit-bearing, examination-requiring, graded, series of three courses in Public Administration, with content somewhat varied at different sites. Successful completion of the program earns a UIC certificate in public administration. Those who score a grade of B or higher in any of the three courses and who subsequently successfully apply for admission to the campus MPA program may have these courses credited toward the degree, as electives. However, the credit offered for the certificate program courses is not automatically considered degree-earning credit.

At two of the above-mentioned sites, the agencies requested more offerings for those who had completed the certificate program. We decided that further UIC education for such individuals would be best accomplished through their seeking admission to our or another degree program. In the meantime, we offered a noncredit on-site management forum for certificate holders only. While trying to be intellectually creative and organizationally innovative, we have also tried to be pedagogically rigorous and correspondingly conservative in the designations we confer in association with such programs.

However, what UIC has chosen to call a certificate program may vary widely from formats for which others will issue "certificates"; has no bearing on "certificates" agencies may issue their own people; involves university credit but not degree credit per se; is unrelated to another extant vehicle, continuing education units of credit; and is unrelated to the "certifications" for which public managers are often eligible from various professional associations and consortia.

It is naive to expect that such usages be standardized across academia, although this would be ideal. However, consortia of academic programs would do well to standardize and discipline their usage of such terminology and the manner in which they sort out their offerings and package possible programs. At the very least, it is imperative that continuing education administrators work to formulate and enforce consistent policies in such matters as regards the offerings within their own institutions. In multiprofessional organizations such as universities, such efforts entail extensive, sensitive negotiation. The continuing education administrator of the coming wave will have to be a campus diplomat, if not a campus politician.

Such policies usually will require executive-level support after they have been discussed by faculty in appropriate forums. The point is that the agenda of interinstitutional relations that the coming wave will bring cannot be jeopardized by maintaining a patchwork of labels, credit policies, trainication ambiguities, and anarchic policy contexts, which invariably favor the pedagogically less disciplined.

Most important, it is wise to sympathetically but clearly resist excessive client demands for various certificates, certifications, credit earnings, and expectations for degree eligibility associated with university-related programs. The trainication mindset is especially likely to generate excessive interest in such documentation as a dividend of participation.

THE THIRD DIMENSION: RESEARCH ASSISTANCE

University faculty generally have research interests that complement their areas of teaching interest, and their training skills, such as they may be, have developed as a by-product of their research and teaching experience. Major universities and their faculties tend to prefer that the use of faculty time in training and educational relationships with external organizations, including government agencies, serve to further faculty research agendas, directly or indirectly.

In the four-stage model of agency-university development described above, it is anticipated that warming external organizations to relationships with universities through satisfying training and educational experiences (once trainication confusions on either side have been eliminated) will lead to a mutual awareness of the value of research relationships.

External organizations will learn that universities can give them state-of-the-art information about the agencies' own workings, the comparative context of their performance, solutions to problems they know they have or suspect they have, the shape of developments to come (from within or without), and the extent to which the issues of concern to them are unique, and not merely instances of broader organizational, governmental, or public policy problems.

University faculty will learn that client organizational environments can be good places for collecting data, testing theories, and answering questions pertaining to their research agendas. The organization of modern universities is such that many faculty pursue their research interests in groups and/or in affiliation with research-focused subunits in the form of institutes, centers, programs, "offices of this and that," and so on, apart from traditional departmental affiliations. These research-focused subunits are often heavily committed to contractually arranged or grant-supported research.

As a result, productive training and, certainly, productive educational relationships between agencies and universities are good platforms for launching a relationship into a more sophisticated orbit: institutionally supported research relationships. Professors, as members of research units, conduct research requiring external agency cooperation. Agencies gain knowledge relevant to their activities; professors get to do their research; universities advance their institutional missions. The financial vehicles of grants and contracts make the relationships feasible, either through a direct relationship between agency and university units or with the partial or total assistance of third-party funding sources.

At this level of the relationship between agency and university there has developed a mutual interest in mutual invigoration. The institutions literally learn from each other—on a long-term basis, and with a considerable investment in each other. From a routine contracting for training in routine matters, the relationship moves to the more profound level of education (at which level the agency is transformed somewhat more than the university) until it becomes a symbiosis in which each party operates at its most important boundary: scholarship at the university and self-examination at the agency.

Practical Issues of Concern at the Initial Stage

At this point in the relationship, tensions can develop, stemming from a gap between agency and university assumptions about the purpose of research. The hesitancy that can cause flight from the relationship on either side stems from the culture gap between academia and the practitioner world regarding evaluation of the research function. Indeed, a substantial literature has developed on this topic (Benveniste, 1977; Horowitz & Katz, 1975; Lerner, 1976a; Wildavsky, 1979).

In briefest terms, the clash of cultures that can derail agency-university relations at this stage has to do with conflicts over confidentiality of data versus client organization access to information about itself; freedom to publish versus the external organization's proprietary rights; research design needs versus agency cost and time issues (on contract research in particular); confining research within practical policy parameters from the outset versus giving full play to the theoretical interests of researchers; and making sense of the financial, procedural, and other uniquely organized aspects of academic research, not to mention the requirements of third-party funding sources.

Organizational differences. In addition, differences between the organizational structures of universities and those of external organizational partners, especially government agencies, can have a sharp impact at this stage of the interorganizational relationship. The typical government agency is a traditional administrative hierarchy of the Weberian type, while the modern university, and especially the research-focused mega-university, may be better understood as a loosely coupled organization, and perhaps, to outside eyes, a veritable "organized anarchy" (see Cohen & March, 1986; Kaplan, 1980; Weick, 1976).

One consequence of this difference is that researchers may become alienated, not to mention frustrated, in starting research and in securing authoritative clarifications and actions from "traditional" organizations. My personal experience suggests that the culture shock is far more severe on the other side: when agency decision-makers confront the organizational maze of universities. A predictable occasion of confusion is the moment the external organizational decision-maker realizes that people in university units unrelated to that of his university counterpart of the moment can also do, perhaps have done, or are at this very moment already doing applied research of the type being contemplated with the current counterpart. People in academic units with seemingly unrelated titles in seemingly different corners of the university, in conjunction with committees, institutes, centers, schools, divisions, departments, programs, and so on, appear to be wandering around the university and the larger environment as independent contractors connected only through an informal, if elaborate, network.

Such realizations may frustrate external decision-makers, leading to the conclusion that the university is a disorganized and hence undesirable partner in research—compared to, say, a consulting company. Alternatively, external actors may sense that they are free to shop around in the system and wander through the university structure as if it were an academic mall, contemplating arrangements with this or that boutique of researchers. The likelihood of competition, resentment, and administrative and subculture complications is considerable. At the same time, the constructive possibilities contingent on mature linkage-building must also be emphasized.

These issues related to structural differences between typically hierarchic-traditional agency organization and typically loose-coupled university organization can be encountered in training and education relations as well. However, it seems that because the latter activities are normally associated with earlier stages of contact, the awareness and sense of possibilities that would underlie an interest in "shopping the university system" have not yet developed on the agency side in the training and education phases.

Continuing education units in liaison. The role of the continuing education unit in the research assistance stage is that of one liaison unit among a cluster of liaison units that are capable of keeping the interorganizational relationship from derailment. As the interorganizational relations of the university in the coming wave reach the complexities of this stage, continuing education is obviously no longer the primary focus of contact between institutions. However, in the loose, often people-focused relations between actors at the boundaries of two institutions, the relationship histories of the actors always figure prominently in the conduct of complicated dialogues. The dominance of the early stages of the relationship by continuing education functions and representatives makes them valuable carriers of institutional memory, as well as trusted actors in the relationship, actors who have already had the opportunity to take a serious and unhurried reading of their interinstitutional counterparts. For these reasons, and also because of their ever-present skills in interinstitutional communication, the continuing education administrators of the coming wave can and must be counted as part of the interinstitutional liaison team of the modern mega-university. Parochially, this means inclusion in executive-level discussion and planning of specific interinstitutional ventures, particularly those that have begun with training and education relationships. We have moved far beyond an evening course in new math taught at the local high school.

Practical Issues in Fostering Inter-organizational Relations: Addressing Research Needs

Frank and thorough discussion, producing absolutely clear under-standings regarding reciprocal rights and responsibilities, must precede the undertaking of research involving contractual relationships, to be sure, but also research involving any acknowledged "informal cooperation." "Infor-mal" is not a synonym for "confused."

In general, university faculty tend to underestimate the degree to which their unit redundancies and overlaps, their overlapping individual roles in various units with multiple reporting lines, and their mixes of teaching, service, research, contract research, grant activity, and personal consulting are difficult for outsiders to fathom, much less anticipate. Moreover, the early stages of such outsider confusion may appear asymptomatic. That is, conversations are vulnerable to hidden misunderstandings of expectations and interests, without this being immediately clear to the participants. They may think they are communicating, whereas they are actually speaking past each other.

Thus, university faculty would do well to accept the responsibility of acting as more than professionals practicing research autonomously through the good offices of their parent institution, somewhat as physicians with staff privileges in the hospitals of the 1960s tended to view their rela-tionships to those hospitals. Rather, faculty should accept the responsibility to function as information and liaison officers on behalf of their institu-tions. Ultimately, all faculty are therefore continuing education faculty in the coming wave. A significant corollary of this is that continuing education administrators should be seeking to establish meaningful relationships with wide networks of faculty, not only with the self-starters who have tradition-ally sought out the continuing education office. The major forms of cur-rency in dealing with faculty at the mega-university of the coming wave are likely to remain flexible seeding funds for research assistance and multidi-mensional consultative activities on behalf of the university, which promise income, career visibility, and research access opportunities. The continuing education administrator's ability to trade in this currency is another asset that can be derived from immersion in the strategic processes of the execu-tive level of the university.

The continuing education administrator will also need to nurture the role of orienting outside parties to the academic professional maze, helping external organizational actors to network in the university. Faculty undertaking such responsibilities have the right to explain their proprietary concerns within the collegial context of their institution, and to expect outsiders being introduced to the university through their liaison efforts to be sensitive to such proprietary concerns as their contacts radiate outward through the university system. Continuing education administrators serving such functions have a similar right to focus, within reason, on their unit's wares, while also providing liaison to other units and actors within the institution as the situation warrants. The continuing education administrator is not the sole liaison actor in a mega-university, but should be viewed, and should view him- or herself, as an essential part of the liaison team.

Major research universities with much overlapping of unit and faculty interests and identities would do well to encourage "soft coordination" of separate dealings with large external clienteles such as government agencies and foundations. All parties have an interest in clarifying the big picture of multiple relationships and projects that are being considered between a large university and a large external client. This interest is in introducing economies and coherent planning, not in reducing points of access or overall relationship flexibility.

However, it is beyond the scope of this chapter to discuss particular approaches to administering such "soft coordination" functions. Suffice it to note that as the research relationship with a government agency or foundation grows, such flexible coordination of multiple contacts and relations between two large organizations is an important consideration, and a relationship dimension to be anticipated and discussed. For the reasons indicated, continuing education should be seen as a component of that relationship system that is valuable to both parties in the relationship.

THE FOURTH DIMENSION: A SHARED, OPEN SYSTEM

The four-stage, normal developmental model for agency-university relations, as described in this chapter, envisions as the last stage an ever-increasing complexity of interaction, what might technically be called a shared, open system. It envisions a relationship dimension that is rich enough to be greater than the sum of its parts (the preceding three levels). A major aspect of this dimension is the development of what may be called an "intellectual salon" atmosphere.

The physical premises of the university units at the core of the university relationship with the agency become a place where agency leaders and their university counterparts may regularly congregate for nonspecific purposes. Periodic gatherings become occasions for fertile shoptalk and camaraderie, and thereby seedbeds for mutually inspired training, education, and research projects.

Within this fourth dimension of agency-university relations, programs can be undertaken to prepare the way for shared, open-system relations and their ultimate manifestation in an intellectual salon atmosphere. However, to succeed, such programs must be carefully developed and nurtured programs in their own right. The development of agency-university relations is a complex process. The best insurance against its failure is the willingness to treat each level of development as a worthy end in itself, while understanding the power of well-functioning levels of relationship to create the possibility of further developments on more sophisticated dimensions.

Here we are concerned once again with the special role that the continuing education unit of the coming wave can play. On this dimension, the linkage of continuing education with conference arrangements, actual conference centers (where possible), and other support services associated with the open-door, open-system atmosphere is a vital linkage that gives full meaning to the continuing education function. Thus is an old structural form revitalized for a new agenda. Continuing education administrators need to reexamine the contribution that conferencing functions can make to their strategic agendas in the context of a reconfiguration of continuing education units to face the coming wave.

The following are descriptions of several worthwhile fourth-dimension programs in which continuing education could play a central role.

Cooperative Education-Work Programs for New Middle-level White-collar Workers

While co-op programs are usually viewed as undergraduate enterprises, their value as a way of upgrading agency management through education should be explored. These programs are continuing education functions in the broadest sense, and for graduate students. They may place students in administrative positions or administrators in graduate programs. They enable students to work half-time and attend graduate school half-time. Time may be divided within each workweek or in terms of half-years. The relevance of such programs to the fourth dimension of agency-university relations as opposed to merely the second dimension (of education) is that continuous interorganizational cross-fertilization, albeit by student managers, is involved. The orientation, support, special servicing, and intrauniversity liaison functions that such programs entail are ideal tasks for the continuing education unit of the coming wave, in coordination with particular sponsoring academic units.

Executive programs. Executive programs in business, public administration, and various professional fields of study constitute another mode
of university relations with external organizations on the fourth dimension.
While not strictly mutual, they bring executive students in contact with
one another and faculty in a customized setting to engage in intellectual
interaction regarding academic, practitioner, and borderline issues in public
administration. The fourth-dimension potential of such programs lies in
the organizational capacity of executives to readily implement, as an extension of their educational discussions with faculty, cooperatively discovered
innovations stemming from their curriculum material. The liaison and contractual capabilities of continuing education units make them ideal key
actors in organizing and administering support services for such programs.

Faculty sabbaticals at agency sites. Faculty sabbaticals, as well as
other part-time release arrangements, can be used to allow university professors to spend considerable blocks of time immersed in the life of government agencies, private corporations, and third-sector organizations. Faculty roles in such capacities may take several guises, including those of
visiting researcher, management consultant, and participant observer. The
network of associations formed by a continuing education unit geared to
the coming wave should make such a unit a useful actor in the establishment
and operation of this sort of program as well.

Administrative "sabbaticals" at university sites. Reciprocally, senior agency, corporate, and third-sector administrative staff may be given
full or partial leaves to spend time at universities for purposes broader than
pursuing degrees or attending classes as nondegree students. They may be
designated visiting fellows (where universities are able to fund and organize
such programs—perhaps on the model of Harvard University's Nieman
Fellows in Journalism), or visiting adjunct faculty, or visiting distinguished
practitioners, who, in the latter case, might be organized in a group whose
activities for a specified period include attending a special seminar with
appropriate faculty and administrators, providing career counseling to students, and perhaps mentoring current or recent graduates already serving
in parallel external organizations.

Again, while continuing education will not be the sole or even lead
actor in university efforts in such arrangements, the continuing education
unit is a valuable contributing unit to a multi-unit effort within universities
with such interests. This is a far cry from the current understanding of the
value of continuing education—an understanding universities cannot afford to leave unmodified in the era of the coming wave. While that era
will offer new opportunities, it will also be less tolerant of mistakes and
lassitude.

Continuing Education and the Fourth Dimension

Various other opportunities for universities developing fourth-dimension relationships also allow continuing education to play a role, again as part of the university's liaison team. Such opportunities include the fostering of program advisory councils in specific professional program areas — in effect, advisory councils regarding continuing education per se.

Reciprocally, corporate and public agency advisory groups on building relations with universities are also interinstitutional vehicles, now initiated from the nonuniversity side, in which continuing education representatives of the university would be valued participants, much as union representatives sit on corporate boards.

Universities can begin the process of opening fourth-dimension relations by establishing advisory councils of practitioners and related third-sector actors for the purpose of bringing faculty and practitioners into periodic dialogue on the subject of university educational and training plans and ventures. Periodic meetings of this type between faculty groups and groups of practitioners with various orientations can foster awareness within the practitioner group as well as the faculty and university administrative group, and of course, mutual awareness between external agencies and the university.

Advisory councils of either type constitute limited, low-cost, and low-risk (in terms of changing institutional cultures) beginnings of fourth-dimension relations — in effect, institutional ice-breakers. Their dividends may include narrower, more issue-specific relationships between individuals and subgroups of individuals from the agency, the university, and the third sector whose first regular contacts began with advisory council participation. Such councils could also become the de facto structure for "meetings of the whole," serving as a unifying thread amid the loosely linked, bilateral relationships originated in council contacts. The continuing education unit of the coming wave should be an adept boundary actor capable of contributing significantly to such efforts.

CONCLUSION AND OVERVIEW

The proper training and education of external organizational citizens must be conceptualized in the context of a clear understanding of the dynamics of interorganizational relations as universities are capable of conducting them, given their loosely linked, multiprofessional structures. Universities can play a significant role in the invigoration of the public service and the private sector. However, the actual significance of this role in the long run is contingent upon the development of mature and robust interorganizational relations that can reach increasingly complex stages. This entails grasping the significance of nurturing relations across two organizational cultures. Mutual empathy in the development of mutually advantageous agendas is the best foundation for productive, multifaceted, long-term cooperation, resulting in general social dividends as well as benefits to the agency and the university, and in success for each side's mission. Successful cooperation requires a talent for working the interorganizational boundary as a proactive member of the university infrastructure. This is the indispensable role of the continuing education unit in the coming wave. As the modern mega-universities will have little choice but to enter such interinstitutional relationships, so the modern continuing education unit will have a clear choice, to be consigned to serving as a purely peripheral unit in a shrinking institution, or to help lead the response to the challenge that the coming wave surely represents.

REFERENCES

Ahn, K., & Saint-Germain, M. (1988). Public administration education and the status of women. *American Review of Public Administration, 18*(3), 297–307.

Benveniste, G. (1977). *The politics of expertise* (2nd ed.). San Francisco: Boyd & Fraser.

Cohen, M., & March, J. (1986). *Leadership and ambiguity: The American college president* (2nd ed.). Boston: Harvard Business School Press.

Horowitz, I., & Katz, J. (1975). *Social science and public policy in the United States*. New York: Praeger.

Jablin, F., Putnam, L., Roberts, K., & Porter, L. (1987). *Handbook of organizational communication: An interdisciplinary perspective*. Newbury Park, CA: Sage.

Kaplan, R. (1980). *Intervention in a loosely organized system: An encounter with non-being: Technical report No. 15*. Greenboro, NC: Center for Creative Leadership.

Lerner, A. (1976a). *The politics of decision making: Strategy, cooperation, and conflict*. Beverly Hills, CA: Sage.

Lerner, A. (1976b). *Experts, politicians, and decisionmaking in the technological society*. Morristown, NJ: General Learning Press.

Lopata, H. (1976). The expertization of everyone and the revolt of the client. *The Sociological Quarterly, 17* (Autumn), 435–447.

Morley, E. (1986). *A practitioner's guide to public sector productivity*. New York: Van Nostrand Reinhold.

Ouchi, W. (1982). *Theory Z: How American business can meet the Japanese challenge*. New York: Avon Books.

Peters, T., & Waterman, R. (1982). *In search of excellence: Lessons from America's best-run companies*. New York: Warner Books.

Schott, R. (1986). The psychological development of adults: Implications for public administration. *Public Administration Review, 46*(6), 657–667.

Shapiro, A. (1985). *Managing professional people: Understanding creative performance.* New York: Free Press.

Stewart, A. (1989). *Team entrepreneurship.* Newbury Park, CA: Sage.

Volker, A. (1989). *Leadership for America: Rebuilding the public service.* Washington, DC: U.S. Government Printing Office.

Weick, K. (1976). Educational organizations as loosely coupled systems. *Administrative Science Quarterly, 21*, 1–19.

Wildavsky, A. (1979). *Speaking truth to power.* Boston: Little, Brown.

Wolf, J. (1983). Career plateauing in the public service: Baby boom and employment bust. *Public Administration Review, 43*(2), 160–165.

Epilogue: Looking Inward

Allan W. Lerner

We have made a considerable effort to analyze features of the coming wave and issues involved in adapting to it. Throughout, continuing education with its functions and structures has been proffered as a potential prime medium of adaptation.

In an epilogue it is common to look ahead. However, it has been the nature of this entire volume to attempt to look ahead. Thus, it would appear more appropriate to end this book by looking within.

A flagship enterprise requires a vessel worthy of being a flagship and recognition of that worthiness by the entire fleet. The crew and equipment must be up to the responsibility. The admiralty must acknowledge this and act accordingly. What human and physical resources must a continuing education unit possess that would merit a leading role in meeting the coming wave? What must the mega-university do to effectively use continuing education as a strategic orientation in dealing with the coming wave?

In order to perform the types of activities described in the preceding chapters, continuing education as a structure would seem to require considerable expertise in a number of areas. Continuing education units of the future that seek a serious level of university underwriting — including money and risk absorption — will have to become professionally adept at marketing research. Those that are already adept will have to extend their role in the comprehension of marketing issues within university administration. Those units that lag behind in this area need to be supported if they are to make the grade.

The term "marketing research" should be broadly construed, in its academic sense, to include research on the opinions and behavior of target groups as these relate to making use of continuing education opportunities. This definition goes beyond attractive mailings about existing offerings. Comprehensive marketing expertise includes the ability to scientifically assess particular programs being advocated within the university, as well as

programs being contemplated in emulation of programs that have suc-
ceeded elsewhere. Marketing expertise is also necessary for taking the pulse
of a potential client group, and for learning how groups network with
related groups. Focus-group techniques, survey research and elite interview-
ing, and follow-up studies and tracking of clients completing a program
are just some of the skills practiced professionally in the corporate world
and taught in our graduate business schools. Ironically, these skills
are rarely practiced by major universities housing such business schools,
when it comes to doing for the university what the university teaches its
students to do for others. Those continuing education programs in the
country that have taken the lead in implementing such technologies need to
be emulated.

The "cobbler's children" syndrome with respect to marketing research
capabilities as well as a host of other sciences in universities is not difficult
or expensive to change when an institution makes a decision to do so.
Particularly when one considers the revenue that can be produced through
such techniques, the cost of upgrading continuing education units in this
regard is not a significant reason for clinging to amateurism.

Public relations capabilities are also needed to effectively meet the
coming wave, and here too continuing education can play a major part.
Contained within continuing education structures, or in service of continuing education as an external unit, it is necessary to spread the word about
continuing education if all the wonderful things it can provide to potential
users are to be made use of by them. Within the university, problems for
which continuing education can provide a remedy are not always automatically diagnosed as such. Senior administrators must be educated to see the
continuing education unit as a life preserver when the coming wave washes
over the institution. If this book has had something new to say to a professional audience, there yet remains the task of getting the word to nonacademic organizations and specialized audiences regarding the benefits of
contact with continuing education units.

Continuing education units in the thick of coping with coming wave
developments will also need state-of-the-art administrative capability. Here
too, the need is for movement away from gifted amateurism—in a sense
the curse of administration in professionalized organizations like hospitals
and universities—and toward the employment of administration professionals. In continuing education administration they will include personnel
with graduate education in public- and private-sector administration, in a
mix that will depend on the public or private character of the institution.

Aggressive program development—indeed, visionary leadership—with
respect to adult learning, interorganizational arrangements for teaching
and field research opportunities, and related funding must come from the

continuing education unit seeking to enact its full potential. As a boundary-spanning entity that should be expected to have the corresponding bicultural awareness, continuing education will have to be able to envision and articulate what it is configured to accomplish.

Unfortunately, as some of the preceding chapters have shown, awareness of continuing education's full potential is frequently undeveloped in particular institutions. In these cases, if the continuing education unit waits to be asked, it will be left high and dry.

The continuing education unit ready to serve its university to the full potential of its function in dealing with a transformed environment will also have to place a high priority on the internal education and absorption of the appropriately gifted faculty within its own institution. They must be identified, cultivated, recruited, and continually developed as much as any external potential client—more so, in fact, as they are harder to replace. They and the heads of their academic units must be shown the strategic potential of continuing education and their interest in its creative uses beyond teaching an extra course for overload payment. The use of continuing education faculty as program development consultants and recruitment consultants would serve several coming wave purposes at once. These purposes include raising the internal salience of continuing education in post-stereotypical terms, generating new venture concepts in peer discussions, the ability to speak the technical language of an external elite in discussions between continuing education and such groups, providing pedagogic grounds for setting format and substance requirements in programs established for particular educational objectives, and the capacity to assess research and research funding potential in specialized areas. In broadest terms, the normalization of continuing education faculty's role will help to absorb continuing education structurally into the strategic policy-making councils of the university. This is the academic administration group at the executive level.

In sum, the overarching issue in the proper utilization of continuing education to make the most of the coming wave is the executive-level absorption of continuing education into the formal and informal processes that constitute the setting of the strategic institutional agenda. Our hope is that this volume will prove inspiring as well as enlightening as regards the nature of the coming wave and the possibilities inherent in riding it to new heights.

About the Contributors

Mark E. Comadena is an Associate Professor in the Department of Communication at Illinois State University. He earned his Ph.D. in communication from Purdue University, his M.A. in communication from West Virginia University, and his B.A. in speech communication from Edinboro State College. Dr. Comadena is currently a research fellow for the Project for the Study of Adult Learning. His research interests focus on the social and psychological factors that affect communication in the classroom, and the effects of classroom interaction on student learning.

Joe F. Donaldson currently serves as Associate Professor in the department of Higher and Adult Education and Foundations at the University of Missouri–Columbia. He earned his Ph.D. in continuing education at the University of Wisconsin–Madison and his B.S. and M.S. degrees at the University of Tennessee–Knoxville. From 1979 to 1983 he was assistant head, and from 1983 to 1987 head, of the Division of Extramural Courses at the University of Illinois at Urbana–Champaign. His research and writing focus on the administration of continuing higher education and on continuing professional education. He is the author of *Managing Credit Programs in Continuing Higher Education*.

Marcia D. Escott currently serves as Director of Adult Learning at Illinois State University. She earned her Ph.D. in Educational Administration and Foundations at Illinois State University and her B.A. and M.A. degrees in English at Ball State University. Recipient of the National University Continuing Education Association (NUCEA) Region IV's Professional Continuing Educator of the Year award, she has served as a consultant and presenter at national, regional, and state conferences and workshops. Her research and publication agenda focuses on communication theory as it relates to the adult learner, teaching strategies, and the development of adult learning programs.

B. Kay King is Director of the Office of Continuing Education and Public Service at the University of Illinois at Chicago and Adjunct Assistant Professor of the Department of Medical Education, College of Medicine. She is responsible for the administration of credit courses, contractual courses, conferences, and noncredit programs sponsored by the 15 colleges and academic units of the campus. Reporting to her are the unit directors of the Office of Conferences and Institutes, the Credit Division, and the Tutorium in Intensive English. She earned her doctorate in adult education from Indiana University.

As an active member of the National Continuing Education Association since 1976, she has served on several committees and offices. A past chair of Region IV, she was recently elected Alternate Representative to the National Board. Her research focuses on the administration of higher continuing education program development.

Allan W. Lerner is Associate Dean of the Graduate College and Professor of Political Science at the University of Illinois at Chicago. In his faculty capacity he also serves as Director of the UIC Graduate Program in Public Administration. He has been active in continuing education instruction and program development, and received the 1990 NUCEA Region IV Faculty Service Award. His areas of academic specialization are organizational theory and politics, and political psychology. His previous books include *The Politics of Decision Making: Strategy, Cooperation, and Conflict; The Manipulators: Personality and Politics in Multiple Perspectives; Public Administration: A Realistic Reinterpretation of Contemporary Public Management* (with John Wanat); and *Public Administration: Scenarios in Public Management* (with John Wanat).

Jovita M. Ross-Gordon currently serves as Assistant Professor and Professor-in-Charge of Adult Education at The Pennsylvania State University. Her B.S. and M.A. degrees were earned at Northwestern University. Her Ed.D. in Adult Education was earned at the University of Georgia. Her research interests focus on adult learning and instruction of diverse groups (reentry women, adults with learning disabilities, adults from ethnic and racial minority groups).

William D. Semlak currently serves as Professor of Communication at Illinois State University. He earned his Ph.D. in speech communication at the University of Minnesota and his B.A. and M.A. at Marquette University. At Illinois State University he has served as Director of Honors (1978–1980), Chair of the Department of Communication (1979–1984), and Acting Chair of the Foreign Language Department (1986–1987). Dr Semlak is currently a research fellow for the Project for the Study of Adult Learning. He has published numerous articles in communication and is author of two books on communication and conflict.

Index

Academic model, 88–91
Access programs, 29–33
Accountability, 103–104, 111, 127
Adam, K., 38
Adams, J. S., 78
Administration, of continuing higher education, 159. *See also* Continuing higher education (CHE) structures; Financial strategies
financial operations in, 104
research on, 68–69
Adult Education (Adult Education Quarterly), 65–66, 72
Adult Education Research Conference (AERC), 65–66, 67
Adult Learning: Research and Practice (Long), 65–66, 67
Advisory councils, 155
African-Americans, 24
access programs for, 32–33
access requirements of, 29–30
career patterns of, 27
college enrollment patterns of, 25–26
earnings ration of, 27–28
Agriculture, land grant institutions and, 51–52, 53
Agyekum, S. K., 65, 67, 68
Ahn, K., 137
Aldrich, H. E., 35
Andersen, J. A., 60
Argyris, C., 39, 40
Asby, W. R., 37
Asian-Americans, 23–24
Aslanian, C. B., 22, 29, 31

Baker, C. O., 22, 27
Beaty, J., 31–32
Bendor, J., 96
Bennis, W. G., 37, 79, 95, 112
Benveniste, G., 149
Black Issues in Higher Education, 30
Blacks. *See* African-Americans
Bloom, B. S., 59
Bohlin, R. M., 128
Boyd, R. H., 69, 73
Boyer, E. L., 50–53, 61–62

Briscoe, D. B., 23
Brokering, research role and, 78–79
Bromley, A. D., 74
Brookfield, S. D., 128
Brown, C. E., 70, 71
Brue, D., 71
Bruno, R., 22, 25
Budgeting. *See* Financial strategies
Bureaucratization as barrier to cross-cultural learning, 40
Burnout, faculty, 55
Bush, G., 54
Bush, V., 74
Business and industry. *See also* Managers
adult education and training programs in, 27
cooperative education-work programs, 153–155
corporate/agency contractual collaboration (CCC) and, 116–120
dependence on continuing higher education programs, 125
quasi-universities of, 126

Cain, R. A., 30
Campbell, D. D., 74–75
Campbell, M. D., 128
Carnegie Commission on Higher Education, 12, 53
Carnevale, A. P., 27
Carroll, D., 22, 24, 26
Carter, D. J., 24, 25
Cervero, R. M., 70
Chiste, K. B., 31–32
Cohen, M., 6, 10, 12–13, 93, 149
Collaboration. *See* Financial planning models
College Board, 24
Comadena, M. E., 4, 49–63, 58–60
Common school movement, 42
Communication style, 59–61
Conger, J. A., 14
Consolini, P., 8–9
Consortium arrangements, 122–124
Consultants, university, 132–136, 160